Understanding Dispensationalism

Understanding Dispensationalism

Mark Sweetnam

WIPF & STOCK · Eugene, Oregon

Wipf and Stock Publishers
199 W 8th Ave, Suite 3
Eugene, OR 97401

Understanding Dispensationalism
By Sweetnam, Mark
Copyright © 2013 by Sweetnam, Mark All rights reserved.
Softcover ISBN-13: 978-1-7252-8932-1
eBook ISBN-13: 978-1-7252-8933-8
Publication date 10/16/2020
Previously published by Scripture Teaching Library (STL), 2013

This edition is a scanned facsimile of the original edition published in 2013.

*Now to the King of the ages, the incorruptible, invisible, only God, honour and glory to the ages of ages.
Amen.*

1 TIMOTHY 1:17 (JND)

*God's ways are behind the scenes:
but He moves all the scenes which
He is behind.*

JOHN NELSON DARBY

Light Shining out of Darkness

God moves in a mysterious way,
   His wonders to perform;
He plants his footsteps in the sea,
   And rides upon the storm.

Deep in unfathomable mines
   Of never failing skill,
He treasures up his bright designs,
   And works His sov'reign will.

Ye fearful saints, fresh courage take,
   The clouds ye so much dread
Are big with mercy, and shall break
   In blessings on your head.

Judge not the Lord by feeble sense,
   But trust Him for His grace;
Behind a frowning providence
   He hides a smiling face.

His purposes will ripen fast,
   Unfolding ev'ry hour;
The bud may have a bitter taste,
   But sweet will be the flow'r.

Blind unbelief is sure to err,
   And scan His work in vain;
God is His own interpreter,
   And He will make it plain.
                    William Cowper

Preface

THIS VOLUME HAD its origin in a series of lessons on the dispensations given to the Rathmines Gospel Hall Sunday School. Teaching this material to children – and adults – of all ages was both a challenge and a privilege, and I am deeply grateful to the overseers in Rathmines for the opportunity to take up the subject. As ever, I am grateful to the boys and girls who rose to the challenge of the material with enthusiasm and vigour.

While preparing and presenting these lessons, it became increasingly clear to me that there was a definite need for a book that introduced dispensational teaching in a systematic but Biblical way. Having complained about this to everyone who would listen, I finally decided to make an attempt to address the need, and it is the fruit of those efforts that you now hold in your hands. It is my hope and prayer that it will encourage God's people to think more often and more carefully about the way in which God has structured history, and His revelation of Himself in history. If its origin in Sunday School is, to some extent a limitation of this book, I trust that it will also be the source of some of its strengths.

Attempting to treat a subject as complex and important as the dispensations is a daunting task, and I am grateful for the encouragement of a number of brethren who generously took the time to read through the manuscript of this volume and comment on it. To order their contributions by value would be impossible, not to say invidious, and so I list them here in alphabetical order: Walter Boyd, Ernest Dover, Stephen Fellowes, David Gilliland, Wesley Martin, David Peden, and Sam Sweetnam. All of these provided helpful comments; none of them can be held responsible for the conclusions I have reached or the way in which I have expressed them.

Very special thanks are due to Sara and to Josiah for their love, encouragement, and support.

DUBLIN, 2013

Contents

	'At Sundry Times and in Divers Manners'	19
1	Ages and Generations	27
2	Dispensations	37
3	The Characteristics of the Dispensations	49
4	The Purpose of the Dispensations	57
5	Continuity in the Dispensations	67
6	Change in the Dispensations	77
7	The Dispensation of Innocence	91
8	The Dispensation of Conscience	109
9	The Dispensation of Human Government	127
10	The Dispensation of Promise	145
11	The Dispensation of Law	167
12	The Dispensation of Grace	191
13	The Dispensation of the Fulness of Times	217
14	Conclusion	231
	Bibliography	235
	Scripture Index	241
	Index	249

Except where otherwise indicated, all quotations from Scripture are taken from the Authorised (King James) Version.

Introduction

'At Sundry Times and in Divers Manners'

The Epistle to the Hebrews deals with some of the grandest and greatest themes of any of the epistles in the New Testament. Fittingly, for a letter that has as its theme the supremacy of Christ, it scales the great heights of God's character and purpose, and takes us right into the presence of God – to the heavenly sanctuary 'not made with hands'. If most writers had been crafting such an epistle, they would have built carefully towards these heights, would gradually have lead their reader higher and higher until they arrived at the climax of their message. That, however, was not the approach taken by the Spirit-guided writer to the Hebrews. Rather, the opening sentence of this epistle catapults us at once to the highest of heights – to God and His purpose for His Son:

> God, Who at sundry times and in divers manners spake in time past unto the fathers by the prophets, hath in these last days spoken unto us by His Son, Whom He hath appointed heir of all things, by Whom also He made the worlds; Who being the brightness of His glory, and the express image of His person, and upholding all things by the word of His

power, when He had by Himself purged our sins, sat down on the right hand of the Majesty on high: being made so much better than the angels, as He hath by inheritance obtained a more excellent name than they (Heb. 1:1–4).

This majestic sentence leaves out no part of God's great plan for His Son; it touches on all the elements of His purpose. Creation, revelation, incarnation, justification and glorification are all included before the writer adds his first full stop. Christ is presented to us as the One Who is essentially and characteristically the Son of God, and Who is at the heart of every facet, every strand of God's eternal purpose.

Each of these subjects contains, in itself, a wealth of truth. But each subject is intricately and inextricably linked with all the others. We cannot speak about Creation without touching on revelation, any discussion of revelation would be incomplete if it did not include the subject of incarnation, incarnation is a vital part of God's plan of justification, and all of these strands have glorification as their ultimate and inevitable goal.

For our present purpose, the way in which these verses present the truths of Creation and revelation is particularly important. Like John 1 and Colossians 1, the other great opening chapters that present us with profound Christological truth, Hebrews 1 emphasises Christ's role in Creation. However, while the other passages present Him as the Creator of a concrete spatial universe – 'all things were made by Him' – Hebrews 1 stresses His role as the Creator of time – 'by Whom also He made the worlds'. As we shall see, the word 'worlds' would be more accurately translated 'ages' – it refers not just to the Creation of the physical universe, but to 'the whole created universe of space and time.'* Thus the Lord Jesus Christ is presented to us here as the Creator of history. Just as He created and ordered the three dimensions of space, so too has He created and ordered the ages of this world.

The opening sentence to Hebrews also has much to say about the plan and pattern of Divine revelation. The writer reminds us that God's revelation of Himself has taken place in time – in those 'ages' created and ordered by Christ. Revelation took place 'at sundry times and in divers manners'. In part, no doubt, the writer is referring to a truth that is obvious to any reader of Scripture. The Bible is not a homogeneous whole; it is marked by a variety of expression, of style, and of genre. It was conveyed at the desk, in the prison, in the desert, and on the mountain top. God communicated in dreams, in visions, and in 'a still small voice'. But this is not the only or the most important truth that this expression conveys. We are also being reminded that God's revelation developed through the centuries. Revelation did not take place all at once – neither Adam and Eve, nor Abraham, nor David, nor any of the great figures of the Old Testament were handed the complete Bible. Instead, God's revelation was partial and progressive, and it built towards the consummation of revelation in the person of Christ, 'in these last days'.

This passage makes it clear, then, that an understanding of the ages, of the 'sundry times' at which God has spoken, is vital to our understanding of Divine revelation. And this epistle provides us with ample evidence of the importance of a chronologically correct

---

* F.F. Bruce, *Commentary on the Epistle to the Hebrews*, (London: Marshall, Morgan & Scott, 1964), 4. William Kelly, *An Exposition of the Epistle to the Hebrews*, (London: T. Weston, 1905) notes 'in general "the ages," but also beyond just dispute used by Hellenistic Jews for the universe (perhaps as the theatre of the Divine dispensations or ages) as here and in Heb. 11: 3' (p. 8).

understanding of Scripture. No other book of the New Testament makes such use of Old Testament Scripture.* The description of the Old Testament as a patchwork revealed 'at sundry times and in divers manners' is emphatically not intended to disparage or denigrate its eternal value as the revelation of God. But the writer goes on to demonstrate the vital importance of a correct understanding of the age in which revelation was given and for which it was given. In his hand, the Old Testament Scriptures that contained the ritual of sacrifice and offering, the ordinance for the Tabernacle, and the order for the Day of Atonement burst into radiant light as he demonstrates the way in which they anticipated and prefigured the person, work, and ongoing ministry of Christ.

This is how it should be. We do not distinguish between the ages so that we might ignore or devalue whole swathes of revelation. Rather the recognition of the distinct and distinctive ages into which God has divided history ought to add value to all of Scripture, as we appreciate the place of each part and piece of revelation in relation to the great pattern imparted to time by its Creator.

These verses make it clear that there is a pattern and a purpose, not just to revelation, but to history itself. We often marvel, and justly, at the wonder of the natural Creation, at its magnificent expanses and its intricate details. Where the Darwinian sees only the blind outworkings of random chance, we see the fingerprints of God. And it is just the same with history. To many, the successive ages of earth are just the accumulation of

---

* Westcott identifies twenty-nine direct quotations of the O.T. in the Epistle, and fifty-three allusions. See Brooke Foss Westcott, *The Epistle To The Hebrews: The Greek Text with Notes and Essays*, (London: Macmillan, 1903), 469–474.

so many random events, meaningless and unstructured. But the believer in the God Who, through His Son, made the ages has a very different perspective. In the passing of the centuries we see the working out of a great and inexorable purpose, and we recognise again, the ordering intellect and the mighty providential power of our God.

This book does not undertake the task of telling the history of dispensationalism. This subject is covered by a large and growing body of popular and scholarly literature, and some suggested readings can be found at the end of this book. Similarly, it is not my purpose to add to the literature that undertakes to defend dispensationalism against its critics. Such efforts are not unimportant and sadly they are far from unnecessary, but they are not our present purpose.

Instead, the purpose of this book is to present the Scriptural truth of the dispensations. Its ambition is to be simple without being simplistic, to introduce the general reader to the wonder of God's plan for the ages, and to demonstrate the way in which a dispensational understanding of the Bible allows us to comprehend better and benefit more from the revelation of God in His word.

If, in doing so, this book appears to present only an academic and technical account of its subject, it will have failed dismally in its purpose. There are few considerations so practical, so vital, or so exhilarating as to trace the great purpose of God through the ages of human history. We love to sing, in the beautiful words of Anne Ross Cousins, of the day when 'I'll bless the hand that guided, I'll bless the heart that planned, when throned where glory dwelleth, in Immanuel's land.' All of us have much cause to thank God that 'our times are in His hand'. But this should be the beginning of our praise and not its conclusion. To rejoice only in the way that God has planned our individual lives is spiritual pettiness of a high order. Would that God might enlarge our hearts and expand our thoughts as we appreciate something of the breath-taking scale of His plan for the ages.

This book will have failed also if it does nothing to rekindle our enthusiasm for God's Word. It must have been a remarkable experience for those to whom the Hebrew epistle was addressed to read it or hear it read for the first time. They knew very well that God had spoken 'unto the fathers by the prophets'. Moreover, they were intimately familiar with the content of the Old Testament. But now they were seeing the Scriptures that they knew so well as though for the first time. What a glorious thing it must have been to realise that they presented Christ in every detail, that, in all the Scripture were 'things concerning Himself'. Getting the dispensations right was no arid scholarship so far as they were concerned. Rather it meant a manifold increase in their understanding and enjoyment of Scripture. It is my prayer that this book, in some small way, may be used of God to enhance the reader's appreciation of the manifold perfections of God's Holy Word.

'Oh that men would praise the LORD for his goodness, and for his wonderful works to the children of men!' (Ps. 107:31). Thus the Psalmist prayed, and no believer can refrain from adding 'Amen!' Alas, we live in a world that, by its wisdom does not know God (1 Cor. 1:21). But those of us who have been saved by grace ought never to cease our praises for the wonder of His works. As we trace God's programme for the history of the universe, the human race, and His people, may our hearts echo the words of the Apostle Paul:

Now unto the King eternal, immortal, invisible, the only wise God, be honour and glory for ever and ever. Amen (1 Tim. 1:17).

Now to the King of the ages, the incorruptible, invisible, only God, honour and glory to the ages of ages. Amen (1 Tim. 1:17, *Darby*).

CHAPTER 1

AGES AND GENERATIONS

HUMAN BEINGS have always puzzled over the meaning of history. We have always had the urge to chronicle and to analyse the events of the past. Anything beyond the most basic effort to understand this record requires us not just to think about events as isolated points in time, but to ask how they fit into a wider picture, how they contribute to the overall trajectory of history. There have been many ideas about the shape of history. Some have understood it as a spiral in which mankind, like a hamster in a wheel, is trapped, condemned to see the same pattern of events endlessly repeated. At more hopeful points in history some optimistic souls have been able to imagine an upward slope. More commonly, though, history has been seen as a downward slope, a slow but inexorable slide towards chaos. Others, particularly today, will scoffingly dismiss every effort to find a pattern in history as mere wishful thinking. They see no overall plan, just a succession of random events and inexplicable catastrophes that toss mankind as savagely and as meaninglessly as a cork in the ocean.

For the believer, none of these options are viable. We are in a position to speak with certainty, for we rely not on the explanations of those whose viewpoint is part of history, but on the account of the Creator of the ages, Who stands outside of time. His Word has much to say about time and history, but one verse is sufficient to outline the true nature of history. Hebrews 9:26 provides us with a panorama of history:

> But now once in the consummation of the ages He has been manifested for the putting away of sin by his sacrifice (*Darby*).

This verse makes it clear that history has a plan. The timing of the first advent of the Lord Jesus Christ was not haphazard. It took place when everything was in place, at the precise moment planned by God.

We learn too that history has a purpose. We are told that the Saviour appeared 'in the consummation of the ages'. Those ages of history that had passed were not just a way of filling time. Rather, they were preparatory. They anticipated the moment of their consummation, the climax of the ages when the seemingly diverse strands of Divine purpose would be drawn together and reach their completion.

It is important to note that the verse refers to the ages. This indicates that history has its periods. We will think about these ages in greater detail shortly but, for now, it is sufficient to notice their existence. History is not presented in this verse as a smoothly continuous stream of time. Rather, God has organised history in discrete and distinctive ages. Each of these ages contributes to the ultimate accomplishment of God's purpose, the working out of His plan.

According to Hebrews 9:28, then, these periods or ages are an important part of God's plan and programme for the history of the universe. To understand them a little more clearly we must think about the word 'ages'. Although many translations, including the King James

Version, translate this word as 'world' it speaks of time, rather than space, of the ages, rather than the planet. The Greek word underlying our English translations is *aiōn* from which we get the English word aeon. Mounce defines *aiōn* as 'a period of time of a significant character; a life; an era; an age'.[*] W.E. Vine's comment on the same word is also worth noting:

> An age, era, signifies a period of indefinite duration, or time viewed in relation to what takes place in that period. The force attached to the word is not so much that of the actual length of a period, but that of a period marked by spiritual or moral characteristics.[†]

We use the word age in a very similar way when we speak of the Stone Age or the Iron Age. When we do so, we are not referring primarily to a period bounded by two dates on the calendar, but of a period characterized by humankind's use of a particular form of technology.

The Bible uses this word in a number of ways. At times it is used to describe 'the conditions and circumstances of earthly existence'[‡] (see, for example, Lk. 20:34). In other places it speaks of the present world in its bondage to sin and Satan – the 'present evil age' (Gal. 1:4) to which we are not to be conformed (Rom. 12:2). The word ages also forms part of two characteristic Scriptural idioms. 'From the ages' means from the beginning of time, while 'to the ages' is usually and accurately translated as 'for ever'. 'To the ages of the

---

[*] William Mounce, Mounce's *Complete Expository Dictionary of Old and New Testament Words*, (Grand Rapids, MI: Zondervan, 2006), 'age', s.v.

[†] W.E. Vine, Expository Dictionary of New Testament Words, (London: Oliphant, 1961), 'age', s.v.

[‡] J.G. T[oll], 'The Ages', *Present Truth*, 2:9.

ages' is a strengthened form, which underpins the King James Version's 'for ever and ever'.

In addition to these usages, the word 'ages' is used in a number of passages that demand further attention. We have already noted that Christ is the Creator of the ages (Heb. 1:2), and that God is spoken of as the 'King of the Ages' (1 Tim. 1:17). In addition, Scripture speaks about the consummation of the ages, the past ages, the present age, and the ages yet to come.

CONSUMMATION OF THE AGES

We have already touched upon Hebrews 9:26. However, while we have noted the importance of the verse, we need to look at its content in a little more detail. It is particularly important to understand what the verse means when it places Christ's death at the 'end of the world', or as it literally translates, at the 'consummation of the ages'. Vine's comment on the word 'end' is helpful:

> [It] signifies 'a bringing to completion together', marking the 'completion' or consummation of the various parts of a scheme. In Mt. 13:39,40,49; 24:3; 28:20, the rendering 'the end of the world' (AV and RV, text) is misleading; the RV marg., 'the consummation of the age,' is correct. The word does not denote a termination, but the heading up of events to the appointed climax. Aion is not the world, but a period or epoch or era in which events take place. In Heb. 9:26, the word translated 'world' (AV) is in the plural, and the phrase is 'the consummation of the ages'. It was at the heading up of all the various epochs appointed by Divine counsels that Christ was manifested (i.e., in His

Incarnation) 'to put away sin by the sacrifice of Himself'.*

In a very wonderful way, this verse reminds us of the centrality of Christ's sin-bearing work to all of time. It is the focal point, the fulcrum of the ages. All of God's actions in past ages worked ineluctably towards it, and all His actions since can be traced back to it. The appearance of Christ, His incarnation and death, are the centre of the purposes of God. It is worth noticing that, a few verses later, the writer reminds us that 'Christ was once offered to bear the sins of many; and unto them that look for him shall he appear the second time without sin unto salvation' (v.28). The first advent of Christ was of unique importance in the great plan of time, and only His second advent, His appearing 'without sin, unto salvation' can compare with its decisive and dramatic impact on this world.

Past Ages

Scripture speaks of the past ages in two distinct ways. Firstly, the communication of Divine revelation throughout human history is stressed. We find this, for example, in the great doxology of Zachariah:

> And his father Zacharias was filled with the Holy Ghost, and prophesied, saying, Blessed be the Lord God of Israel; for He hath visited and redeemed His people, and hath raised up an horn of salvation for us in the house of His servant David; as He spake by the mouth of his holy prophets, which have been since the world [age] began (Lk. 1:67–70).

At this momentous point in the history of the world, as the forerunner of the Messiah is introduced, as God

---

* Vine, *Expository Dictionary*, 'end', s.v.

positions the stage of history for the entrance of His Son in the mystery of incarnation, the inspired words of the old priest remind us that this was no innovation – since the age began, the prophets had spoken concerning the redemption of God's people and the deliverance of Israel. The content of their prophecy helps us to identify the age in question. The earliest prophecy promised the Seed of the woman Who would 'bruise the head of the serpent' (Gen. 3:15), but that anticipated a global rather than a national deliverance. Here, the prophecies spoken of clearly have relevance for Israel. Zachariah looks back over the dispensation whose end was drawing so very close, and rejoices in the fulfilment of God's prophesied plan. Later, at a point no less momentous, Peter spoke of the ascended Christ 'Whom the heaven must receive until the times of restitution of all things, which God hath spoken by the mouth of all his holy prophets since the world [age] began' (Acts 3:21).

Secondly, even while Scripture stresses the revelation given in a past age, it also emphasizes the limitations of that revelation. So, the Apostle Paul wrote to the believers in Colosse of his stewardship of 'the mystery which hath been hid from ages and from generations, but now is made manifest to his saints' (Col. 1:26). So, while the prophets communicated Divine truth in past ages, they proclaimed only a partial revelation. God's people in this present age have been privileged to be the recipients of a revelation that was unknown to past ages.

Present Age

The term age is also used to describe the present. When it is used in this way, it emphasizes the unique character of this age in contrast to those that have preceded and will succeed it.

In Matthew 28:20, the present age is associated with a unique promise. The Saviour is giving to His disciples a foundational commission to go and 'teach all nations, baptizing them in the name of the Father, and of the Son, and of the Holy Ghost: teaching them to observe all things whatsoever I have commanded you' (vv.19–20). This was a task of daunting scale, but even as He commissioned His disciples, He reminded them that He had the power to enable them for it. 'All power' 'in Heaven and in earth' was His, and that resource would support and sustain His servants as they set out to do His work. But that resource – formidable though it was – was not the only one on which they could rely. Along with His power, the Saviour promised His presence – 'lo, I am with you alway, even unto the end of the world [age]' (v.20). This promise holds good for us today. Such a promise was given to no other age. We, the believers of this age, uniquely in all of history have the promise of the Saviour's unfailing unchanging presence with us, 'even unto the end of the age'.

Such a promise distinguishes any age. But 1 Corinthians 10:11 further emphasizes the remarkable nature of the present age. In it, we discover that the present age has a unique perspective:

> Now all these things happened unto them for ensamples: and they are written for our admonition, upon whom the ends of the world [age] are come. (1 Cor. 10:11)

In this verse, the believers of this dispensation are described, along with Paul and the Christians at Corinth as those upon whom the 'ends of the world' are come. Vine highlights two relevant senses of the word end in this context:

> [The word] signifies 'the final issue or result' of a state or process, ... 'a fulfillment,' ... 'the utmost degree' of an act, ... 'the aim or purpose' of a thing.

This verse sheds a dramatic light upon the nature of the present age. It is the age towards which all others have been moving, the climax of history. What a privilege we have to live in this age, and to be able to understand, in a way in which Old Testament believers never could, the full-orbed truth of God's programme. We stand on the summit of the ages, with a vast panorama spread out on every hand. We see the pattern, the progression, and the perfection of the course God marked out for the ages. And yet, we are all too preoccupied with the few square feet on which we stand. Let us leave aside our spiritual myopia, and, taking the telescope of God's infallible Word, lift up our eyes, and scan the far horizons, and worship, with a fresh sense of wonder, the mighty God Who planned and executed it all.

FUTURE AGES

One of the most significant of the Scriptures that refer to the future ages wonderfully confirms the unique importance of the believers of this age in the purposes of God. So, writing to the Ephesians, the Apostle Paul reminds the believers of God's great purpose in their salvation from their past manner of life, and their addition to the Church:

> That in the ages to come He might shew the exceeding riches of His grace in His kindness toward us through Christ Jesus. (Eph 2:7)

The Apostle looks forward beyond the end of the present age, and rejoices in God's purpose to eternally demonstrate His grace and kindness by means of those who never deserved His mercy or His grace. Men and angels, alike, will wonder as they see what God's grace has done, how He has 'raised the ruined wrecks of sin above created thought'.* Paul develops this theme in the following chapter and, as we sound with him the depths of Divine wisdom and scale the heights of Divine power we can scarcely fail to join with him in the doxology that draws the chapter to a close:

> Now unto him that is able to do exceeding abundantly above all that we ask or think, according to the power that worketh in us, Unto him be glory in the church by Christ Jesus throughout all ages, world without end. Amen (Eph. 3:20–21).

GENERATIONS

We have already seen that Paul wrote to the Colossian believers of 'the mystery which hath been hid from ages and from generations, but now is made manifest to his saints' (Col. 1:26). This verse introduces another word that is used in Scripture to describe the divisions of time. The word generations is *'genea'*, from which we get our word genealogy – literally the knowledge of the generations. Most often, it is used in Scripture to speak of generations in the normal sense. It is also used, in a more specific sense to describe the Jewish nation in their rejection of Christ – the Saviour rebuked 'an evil and adulterous generation' (Mt. 12:39) and Peter implored his hearers to save themselves 'from this untoward generation' (Acts 2:40).

In addition to these usages, and as their linkage in Colossians 1 indicates, the word 'generation' is also used in a very similar way to 'ages'. In Acts 14, Paul and Barnabas rebuked the idolatry of the men of Lycaonia, providing them with an overview of God's dealings with mankind:

---

* John Dickie, 'What is the foulest thing on earth?', in *The Gospel Hymnbook*, (Kilmarnock: John Ritchie, 2009), No. 335.

> Sirs, why do ye these things? We also are men of like passions with you, and preach unto you that ye should turn from these vanities unto the living God, which made heaven, and earth, and the sea, and all things that are therein: Who in times [generations] past suffered all nations to walk in their own ways. Nevertheless He left not Himself without witness, in that He did good, and gave us rain from heaven, and fruitful seasons, filling our hearts with food and gladness (Acts 14:15–17).

These verses are of crucial importance for our study. The missionaries outline development in the way in which God has dealt with mankind. His administration of the world in past generations had specific implications for His relationship with the nations. This has now been changed. Paul and Barnabas bring a new message, and one that reveals a new approach to God's dealings with mankind. In Ephesians 3, Paul used the term to express precisely the same points:

> Whereby, when ye read, ye may understand my knowledge in the mystery of Christ) Which in other ages [generations] was not made known unto the sons of men, as it is now revealed unto his holy apostles and prophets by the Spirit. (Eph 3:4–5)

We will examine this development in Divine administration in detail in a later chapter, but it is sufficient for the present to notice the chief features of these verses – history is divided into discrete ages, and these generations have been marked by differences in Divine administration, and those differences are closely linked to God's revelation of Himself to mankind.

CHAPTER 2

DISPENSATIONS

HUMAN HISTORY, as we have seen, is divided into ages and generations. These terms are normal words, and though used in a specific and special way, are not difficult to understand. However, we now have to turn our attention to a less familiar and more technical term that is central to our understanding of God's programme for the ages: dispensation. This is not an everyday word. The common word it most closely resembles is dispenser, but it seems very difficult to trace a link between the device that squirts soap on to our hands in the bathroom and God's grand scheme of organisation for the ages. Nor does an English dictionary provide much enlightenment. The *Oxford English Dictionary* defines the word as 'the action of dealing out or distributing', but this makes it clear that we need to know who is dealing what before we can make any sense of the word. Because this word is so central to our consideration, it is worth our while to consider its meaning in some detail. In this chapter, we will begin by looking at the Greek words that underlie the English translation 'dispensation'. By understanding the concepts associated with these words, we can grasp a good deal of the meaning contained in the word 'dispensation'. Then we will look at the ways in which the word is used in Scripture. Finally, we will attempt to pull these strands together into a definition of this important term.

DISPENSATIONS

This is a vital word to our understanding of God's purpose for the ages. In spite of this, the word 'dispensation' appears only twice in the English New Testament. There are a number of related Greek words that are relevant to our understanding of the concept. The verb *oikonomeō* appears once, in Luke 16:2, and is translated 'to be a steward'. The noun *oikonomos* occurs ten times (Lk. 12:42; Lk. 16:1, 3, 8; Rom. 16:23; 1 Cor. 4:1, 2; Gal. 4:2; Tit. 1:7; 1 Pet. 4:10). It is translated steward, chamberlain, and governor. The noun *oikonomia* is used nine times (Lk. 16:2, 3, 4; 1 Cor. 9:17; Eph. 1:10; 3:2, 9; Col. 1:25; 1 Tim. 1:4) and is translated stewardship and dispensation.

It is from these words that we get our word economy. As this suggests, they speak of order, administration, and stewardship. They imply three things – a master or authority who delegates (the source of the administration), an administration that is delegated (the content of that administration) and a servant or servants who are the responsible recipients of that authority.

These three components are elaborated further when we consider *oikonomia* more closely. It is made up of two other words – *oikos*, meaning house, and *nomos* meaning law (when we speak of an autonomous body we mean one that provides a law, *nomos*, for itself). Each of these components is important for our understanding of the concept of the dispensations.

Firstly, the term *oikos* reminds us of the rights of the householder. The owner of a house has rights in his own home that he does not enjoy in anyone else's. For example, there are some people who request that their guests remove their shoes before entering their home. It would be the height of bad manners for me to refuse to comply with that rule, however reluctant I might be to expose my socks. And, while it is reasonable for those householders to make that request of me as I enter their home, they would receive a decidedly negative response if, when visiting my house, they tried to insist that I must remove my shoes. Ownership of the house imparts unique rights. It is precisely this point that Paul makes in 1 Timothy 3:15, as he instructs Timothy how 'thou oughtest to behave thyself in the house of God'. In God's house, God's rules apply, and Timothy is not at liberty to comport himself as he wills. It is so with the dispensations. In ordering the ages, God acts with creatorial and proprietorial rights. We may not always understand His actions, but we cannot question them, or deny His absolute right to order His Creation as He chooses. The right of God to order and reorder His Creation is at the heart of the concept of the dispensations.

Secondly, the fact that the householder has rights means that the servant has responsibilities. If the master desires that things be done in a certain way, then the servant is responsible to ensure that his wishes are carried out. It is this idea of responsibility that is in the foreground when the work *oikonomia* is translated by 'stewardship'. This relationship is well illustrated for us in Hebrews 3:5–6:

> And Moses verily was faithful in all His house, as a servant, for a testimony of those things which were to be spoken after; but Christ as a son over His own house; whose house are we, if we hold fast the confidence and the rejoicing of the hope firm unto the end.

Christ is a son over His own house therefore He has rights. Moses was a servant in God's house, and thus had responsibilities that he faithfully discharged. Another helpful illustration is provided in Romans 14. In this passage, Paul is, among other things, stating the principle that the servant is responsible only to his own master:

> Who art thou that judgest another man's servant? to his own master he standeth or falleth. Yea, he shall be holden up: for God is able to make him stand (Rom. 14:4).

Paul uses an unusual word for 'servant' here. It is the word *oiketēs*, which has as its root *oikos*. This word, which is used on only five occasions in the New Testament, means a household servant. Paul uses it here, rather than the more common *doulos* (bondservant) or *diakonos* (a minister) because he is making a very specific point about the servant's responsibility to his own master in his own house. The household is the sphere of responsibility, and the idea of responsibility is a vital part of the concept of the dispensation.

Thirdly, *oikonomia* speaks of revelation. *Nomos* is the word normally translated 'law' and it reminds us that administration must be based upon revelation. Unless the master makes it clear how he wishes his house to be administered, the servant has a hopeless task. The principles of administration must be made known. Each dispensation, as we shall see, involves just such a revelation – God, in each successive age, makes known the principles by which He expects men to operate.

These concepts – rights, responsibility, and revelation – are built into the meaning of *oikonomia* and its related words. We have an excellent demonstration of this in the two occasions in the gospels when these words are used. In Luke 12 and 16 the Lord Jesus Christ tells parables that feature stewards and stewardship. In each of these passages, the right of the master of the house to administer his house as he wishes is clear:

> And the Lord said, Who then is that faithful and wise steward [*oikonomos*], whom his lord shall make ruler over his household, to give them their portion of meat in due season? (Lk. 12:42)

> And He said also unto His disciples, There was a certain rich man, which had a steward [*oikonomos*]; and the same was accused unto him that he had wasted his goods. And he called him, and said unto him, How is it that I hear this of thee? give an account of thy stewardship [*oikonomia*]; for thou mayest be no longer steward [*oikonomeō*] (Lk. 16:1–2).

In the second of the passages quoted, we have a clear demonstration of the steward's responsibility towards his master, and the parable in Lk. 12 provides us with an equally clear instance:

> But and if that servant say in his heart, My lord delayeth his coming; and shall begin to beat the menservants and maidens, and to eat and drink, and to be drunken; the lord of that servant will come in a day when he looketh not for him, and at an hour when he is not aware, and will cut him in sunder, and will appoint him his portion with the unbelievers (Lk. 12:45–46).

Implicit in both passages is the idea that the master has made known the rule that he wishes to be obeyed in his house. This is what makes both of these unfaithful stewards so culpable – they both knew what their master expected, and fell short of his expectations. It is worth noting that both of these parables deal not only with stewardship but with its failure, and with the judgement that comes as a result of that failure. These as we will see, are common features of man's response when entrusted with responsibility by his Creator.

With one exception (1 Pet. 4:10) every other occurrence of *oikonomia* and related words is found in the writings of the Apostle Paul. On a number of occasions he uses the word to describe the way in which God has entrusted him with the stewardship of the gospel message:

> For if I do this thing willingly, I have a reward: but if against my will, a dispensation of the gospel is committed unto me (1 Cor. 9:17).

> Whereof I am made a minister, according to the dispensation of God which is given to me for you, to fulfil the word of God (Col. 1:25).

> Let a man so account of us, as of the ministers of Christ, and stewards of the mysteries of God (1 Cor. 4:1).

In a number of other instances, though, Paul uses these words in a different way. These verses are crucial to understanding the wider meaning of the dispensations. Ephesians 1 provides one important example:

> That in the dispensation of the fulness of times He might gather together in one all things in Christ, both which are in heaven, and which are on earth; even in Him: in whom also we have obtained an inheritance, being predestinated according to the purpose of Him who worketh all things after the counsel of his own will: That we should be to the praise of his glory, who first trusted in Christ (Eph. 1:10–12).

Here, the 'dispensation of the fulness of times' looks forward to a future time period that will be marked by a particular type of administration as all things, in heaven and in earth, are gathered together in Christ. God's rights in arranging such a dispensation are stressed here – He gathers, He arranges, He administers.

In Ephesians 3, Paul uses the term in relation to the present age:

> If ye have heard of the dispensation of the grace of God which is given me to you-ward: how that by revelation he made known unto me the mystery; (as I wrote afore in few words, whereby, when ye read, ye may understand my knowledge in the mystery of Christ) which in other ages was not made known unto the sons of men, as it is now revealed unto his holy apostles and prophets by the Spirit; that the Gentiles should be fellowheirs, and of the same body, and partakers of his promise in Christ by the gospel: Whereof I was made a minister, according to the gift of the grace of God given unto me by the effectual working of his power (Eph. 3:2–7).

In this passage, Paul is God's messenger to the Ephesians. He communicates to them the truth that there is a new administration – 'the dispensation of the grace of God' – which stands in contrast to all that went before, 'in other ages'. Paul emphasises the revelation associated with the dispensation. This dispensation of grace was revealed by God to Paul, and by Paul to the believers at Ephesus. God is the dispenser, and it is revelation of the mystery that is dispensed. The recipients of this dispensation – those who have responsibility under it – are the believers of this age – it is 'youward'.

In Colossians 1 we get a very similar picture of the meaning of dispensation:

> Whereof I am made a minister, according to the dispensation of God which is given to me for you, to fulfil the word of God; even the mystery which hath been hid from ages and from generations, but now is made manifest to His saints... (Col.1:25–26).

We have the same order – God dispenses 'to His saints'. We have the same emphasis on revelation – the dispensation of which Paul is a minister was 'hid from ages and from generations', but is now made manifest to His saints. The revelation of this dispensation is said 'to fulfil the word of God'. As Paul stresses, this is not something found already in Scripture – it is the subject of an additional and a completing revelation.

There is another common thread in these passages that we would do well to note with some care. In each of these passages, we learn that there is an intimate link between dispensations and ages. In Ephesians 1, we have a period of time, 'the fulness of times', and a dispensation appropriate for that period. Similarly, in Ephesians 3, we have a dispensation that was not in operation 'in other ages', but which does operate in the present age. And, in Colossians 1, we learn again that the dispensation that Paul describes is not linked with the past ages, but with the present.

This is a point worth stressing. Critics of dispensational theology sometimes complain that dispensationalists use the word *oikonomos* to describe periods of time in history. They point out that the word has no element of time in it, that it speaks of stewardship and not any chronological period. This is true. But stewardships operate in time. The master of the unfaithful steward in Luke 16 could, after he had dismissed him, think back to events that took place during the stewardship of so-and-so. In a very similar way, commentators speak of the Bush administration or the Obama administration and, even though the word administration does not contain any idea of time, we understand that they mean the period characterised by a particular administration, by a particular approach to the issues of government. We might remember, from the previous chapter that:

> An age, era, signifies a period of indefinite duration, or time viewed in relation to what takes place in that period. The force attached to the word is not so much that of the actual length of a period, but that of a period marked by spiritual or moral characteristics.

When, then, we use the word 'dispensation' to describe a period of time, we are stressing 'the spiritual and moral characteristics' that predominate in that age.

Definition

In this chapter, we have considered the concepts contained within the term *oikonomia*. We have seen that it implies the source, the content, and the recipients of a Divinely mandated administration. We have noted that the etymology of the word stresses the rights of the source, the revelation of the content, and the responsibility of the recipients. We have seen these elements in action in the various passages of Scripture that use *oikonomia* and its related terms. We have also noted, from these passages, that administration happens in time and that, therefore, *oikonomia* is associated with the ages into which God has divided history.

It is now time to gather these strands together into a working definition of the term 'dispensation'. Many definitions of the term have been attempted, all stressing broadly the same features of the concept. I am not reusing these, not because they do not do a good job (in general they do) or because there is any value in novelty.

However, it is useful to base our definition as closely as possible on the material covered in this chapter. We can summarise this chapter and define the term dispensation like this:

> A dispensation is a distinct stage in God's |progressive revelation of Himself to mankind. Each dispensation is marked by a distinctive approach to the government of humanity chosen by God, in His sovereignty, for a given period of history and revealed to mankind, making them responsible to obey that revelation.

IMPLICATIONS

This has been a rather technical chapter. That is unavoidable – any attempt to understand the dispensations of Scripture is most likely to succeed if it starts from these first principles. However, there is no doctrine of Scripture that does not have important practical implications, and this is certainly true of dispensational truth. Grasping the nature of God's dealings with humanity has profound implications for our view of God, of mankind, and of Scripture.

As we have seen, the study of the dispensations emphasises the sovereignty of God. As we reflect on the different administrations that He has adopted in different ages, we must acknowledge His rights as the Creator of the universe and the Organiser of time. As well as His sovereignty, we must acknowledge His providence. The successive dispensations are not the evidence of a God Who is repeatedly trying out schemes of administration until He finds one that works. Nothing could be further from the truth. Every detail of every dispensation is known to Him already, and their sequence and succession alike are the working out of His tremendous plan for the ages. We learn too that God is interested in His Creation. He is neither the blind watchmaker of random chance or the distant and disinterested God of Theism. Rather, He has an intimate interest in the work of His hands, and a great purpose in view for all of Creation. We also learn that God is a God of order. The dispensations involve different modes of administration, but nonetheless they all do involve administration. God is not the author of confusion or chaos. The dispensations teach us that He always delights in discipline, dignity, and order.

Considering the dispensations also has implications for our view of humanity. Contemporary thought is thoroughly confused about the place of humanity. It cannot reconcile its insistence on the primacy and autonomy of humanity with its fundamental belief that we occupy our place at the top of the tree of species because of sheer evolutionary good luck. It ends up with a hopelessly schizophrenic and incoherent view of mankind. And this view ultimately debases mankind. We become egotistical and self-indulgent evolutionary bullies, our existence as meaningless as smoke in the wind. This view of mankind owes nothing to God's Word. There, in the pages of Scripture, we learn of the dignity of mankind. We learn that we are the stewards of God, with an authority over Creation devolved from Him. With this great privilege comes corresponding responsibility and it is undeniable that the height of humanity's calling is matched only by the depths to which it has sunk in its failure to discharge the responsibilities of that calling. Nonetheless, an appreciation of the dignity and responsibility that rest upon this unique race will transform our view of society and of our fellow human beings.

Finally, the dispensations have a vital and radical impact on our understanding of Scripture. They are not, nor should they ever become an excuse for partitioning off sections of our Bible – all of God's people at all times need all of God's Word. Reading Scripture from a dispensational standpoint should have precisely the opposite effect. As we grasp the framework of revelation, we understand how the different parts of Scripture fit together. We find apparent contradictions dissolving, and new perfections emerging before our eyes. This is not to suggest that only dispensationalists can enjoy their Bibles – that would be hermeneutical hubris of the highest order. Nevertheless, an understanding of the dispensations and the consequent ability rightly to 'divide the word of truth' (2 Tim. 2:15) do allow Scripture to speak to us on its own terms.

CHAPTER 3

THE CHARACTERISTICS OF THE DISPENSATIONS

IN PREVIOUS CHAPTERS we learned that history has been created by God, not as a uniform or homogeneous flow of time, but as a succession of ages. These ages, we have seen, are distinct periods, each marked by its own particular characteristics. These periods have been ordered and orchestrated by God to conform with His eternal purpose. In each of these ages God adopts a different way of dealing with mankind and these administrations are called dispensations. Having established all this, we now need to ask what dispensations have been in force at which periods in human history. What does a dispensation look like, and how can we recognise them in Scripture?

It is important to begin by acknowledging that there is no portion of Scripture that explicitly lists or outlines the dispensations for us. This should not dismay us too much – the same is true of all manner of great and fundamental truths. So, for example, not only is there no single verse that outlines the truth of the Trinity, the word does not even appear in our Bible. However, the truth is undeniably there, and elements of it can be found in many parts of Scripture. The task of the careful student of Scripture is to grasp the truth of all these portions, and to synthesise them into a comprehensive understanding of the subject. So it is with the dispensations.

On the other hand, the lack of a single verse or passage outlining the dispensations should make us proceed with care. It is vital that our dispensational outline be inferred from Scripture and not imposed upon it. There is a temptation to construct a simplistic grid into which all Scripture must be forced, regardless of how well – or how poorly – it may fit. This is never a satisfactory approach to understanding God's Word. It is imperative that we allow Scripture to guide us in its interpretation. As we approach Scripture, in search of the dispensations, we must remember that we are looking for a discrete period of time marked by a distinctive administration. The inauguration of that new administration always involves a distinct act of revelation on God's part, and this can sometimes make it easier to recognise the beginning of a new dispensation than it is to identify the end of an old one. Not all of the details outlined below will be the subject of unanimous agreement. This chapter provides an overview, and leaves some of the more problematic questions to be addressed in later chapters.

The first dispensation is not difficult to find – it fairly jumps off the page at us. Beyond question, the time spent in the garden of Eden by Adam and Eve was distinctive. Their experience as unfallen human beings, able freely to enjoy the presence of God was unique, entirely unparalleled in the later history of the human race. To recognise this period as a distinct age, marked by a distinct dispensation is certainly not imposition on Scripture, but a clear inference from it.

The Fall of man marked the end of this unique state of being, and so the end of the first dispensation. This event was followed by another period in which humanity existed under a very different form of Divine administration, with the light of conscience to guide its behaviour. While some of the details of this arrangement cannot be said to have come to an end, we find that, after the Flood, God enters into a new relationship with Noah. Thus, the Flood – a cataclysmic global judgement that changed the whole face of Creation – marks the end of the second dispensation.

After the Flood, we find a new word introduced into the lexicon of Scripture. This word – covenant – has important and far-reaching implications that will merit our further consideration, but for the present, it is sufficient to note that the making of this covenant represented the commencement of a new dispensation – God was revealing to Noah some of the principles that would underpin life in this, the first postdiluvian age. This administration continues until we arrive at Genesis 10 and 11. Genesis 10:5 reveals that a dramatic change has taken place in the administration of the earth with the emergence, for the first time, of nations. Genesis 11 explains how this change came about – these nations are a result of the judgement on the tower of Babel. Thus, this judgement brings the third dispensation to an end.

This administration was succeeded by a very different one. In Genesis 12, we find God moving again in revelation. This time, He does not speak to all of humanity (as He did in the garden of Eden) or to a representative of humanity (as He did in the making of the Noahic covenant). Now, He chooses one man, one family, and ultimately one nation, as He enters into another covenant, this time with Abraham.

As we read onwards through Scripture from Genesis 12, the next major act of revelation by God is hardly difficult to identify. At Sinai, amidst the 'fire, ... blackness, and darkness, and tempest' (Heb. 12:18) God inaugurated a new stage in Divine revelation and a new stage in human existence. The Mosaic Law, in all its detail and all its rigour, was now the basis on which God dealt with mankind. And it remained in force, until it was superseded by the One Who is 'the end of the law' (Rom. 10:4).

So many wonderful revelations cluster around the first coming of the Lord Jesus Christ that it is difficult to be dogmatic about the precise moment when a new dispensation might be said to have commenced. Was it at His birth or during His lifetime? We are told that 'grace and truth came by Jesus Christ' (Jn 1:17). Was it in the upper room, where He spoke of the 'blood of the new testament, which is shed for many for the remission of sins' (Mt. 26:28)? Or was it, perhaps, at Calvary, perhaps at that climactic moment when 'the veil of the Temple was rent in twain from the top to the bottom' (Mt. 27:51)? Undoubtedly, these were all very remarkable moments of revelation. However, it will help us if we remember that dispensations are about Divine administration – the arrival of a new dispensation is always heralded by the inauguration of a new way in which God deals with humanity. With this criterion in mind, it seems clear that the day of Pentecost is of particular importance. On that day, the Spirit was given and the Church was formed. God began a new – and very distinct – chapter in the story of His dealings with Creation. In the previous chapter we looked at Ephesians 3, and saw that it spoke of the Apostle as the communicator of the 'dispensation of grace'. Thus, Scripture not only identifies the present as a distinctive dispensation, it also gives us a name for it!

This dispensation is still in operation. The revelation of the next stage in the Divine programme will be dramatic indeed: 'then shall they see the Son of man coming in a cloud with power and great glory' (Lk. 21:27), dramatically bursting into time, to banish rebellion and to establish His kingdom. Once again, Scripture speaks explicitly of this dispensation:

> That in the dispensation of the fulness of times He might gather together in one all things in Christ, both which are in heaven, and which are on earth; even in Him (Eph. 1:10).

This, the dispensation of the fulness of times, is congruent with the Millennial Kingdom of Christ. At its close, time will end, and with it the dispensations that have characterised God's dealings with humanity throughout the history of the world. This is not to say that Divine administration will end. We know relatively little about the detail of the eternal state, but we do know that it will be marked by order and administration. However, it is not a dispensation, in the sense outlined in this chapter because man is not being tested in the same way. As Erich Sauer points out, the eternal state 'does not properly belong to the *unfolding* of salvation, but its *goal* and is therefore not "history but eternity".'[*]

To summarise, then, by focusing on crucial moments of Divine revelation, we have identified seven dispensations in Scripture. The first begins in Eden, and ends with the expulsion of Adam and Eve. The second begins with Adam and Eve outside the garden, and ends with the Flood. The third dispensation begins with God's covenant with Noah, and concludes at the tower of Babel. The fourth dispensation begins with the calling of Abram, and continues until the giving of the Law. The dispensation of Law continues until the death of Christ, and the giving of the Spirit at Pentecost inaugurates the present dispensation – the dispensation of grace. Following the events of the Tribulation, the

---

[*] Erich Sauer, *From Eternity to Eternity*, (London: Paternoster Press, 1954), 70

dispensation of the fulness of times, the millennial reign of Christ will be the final and closing dispensation.

When we look at this list of dispensations, we realise that they share something in common in addition to Divine revelation. The first dispensation begins with God speaking, and ends with the judgement of Adam and Eve. Again God speaks, and again, the judgement of the Flood brings the dispensation to an end. After the Flood, God speaks, and again, the dispensation ends with judgement. God speaks to Abram, and, by the time the dispensation closes, Israel is judged in Egyptian bondage, and that mighty nation, too, bears the brunt of Divine judgement. God speaks at Sinai, and the dispensation of Law stretches through more than seventeen centuries. At its end, severe judgement fell upon the nation and the city that had rejected the Messiah, culminating in the Roman invasion of AD 70, the destruction of the Temple, and the end of the Levitical order. This present dispensation will end in judgement, in 'great tribulation, such as was not since the beginning of the world to this time, no, nor ever shall be' (Mt. 24:21). Finally, the Millennium, too, will end in judgement, as the armies of Satan, in one last desperate attempt to thwart Divine purpose, gather about Jerusalem:

> And they went up on the breadth of the earth, and compassed the camp of the saints about, and the beloved city: and fire came down from God out of heaven, and devoured them. And the devil that deceived them was cast into the lake of fire and brimstone, where the beast and the false prophet are, and shall be tormented day and night for ever and ever (Rev. 20:9–10).

We have laboured this point. But it has been worthwhile to do so. It is fundamental to our understanding of the dispensations to grasp the fact that they begin with revelation. Equally, it is vital to understand that they each end in judgement. Thus, we have revelation and judgement as two of the defining characteristics of a dispensation. But these judgements can only be accounted for as the results of human failure, and so that must be a third characteristic. And, if there be human failure, it implies that there is some responsibility that has not been discharged. Bringing all this together, we can confidently identify four key characteristics of each dispensation:

- Revelation
- Responsibility
- Rebellion
- Retribution.

These four characteristics will provide an invaluable structure for our more detailed consideration of each dispensation in subsequent chapters.

Dispensationalists are often accused of imposing a rigid interpretative scheme of their own concocting upon Scripture. This is a serious charge and would, if true, be a fundamental objection to this approach to Scripture. However, this chapter has demonstrated that this need not, and should not, be the case. It does not take a terribly skilled Scriptural sleuth to follow the clues of the dispensations. This is not an esoteric scheme, dreamed up by men, and crow-barred willy-nilly into the Word of God. As we apply it, we need to ensure that this continues to be the case. It is tempting to oversimplify the dispensations, to make them into neat and watertight compartments. In following chapters, we will see that this is not a tenable approach to understanding Scripture. Its reductionism does lead to a very 'chopological' (to borrow a word from William

Tyndale) exegesis of Scripture.* In seeking to understand the truth of God's inerrant and eternal Word, let us allow Him 'to be His own interpreter' and to make His meaning plain.

---

* William Tyndale, *The Obedience of the Christian Man*, ed. David Daniell (Harmondsworth: Penguin, 2000), 156.

CHAPTER 4

THE PURPOSE OF THE DISPENSATIONS

WE HAVE SEEN that God has divided the history of the world into discrete periods or ages, and has allotted to each age a distinctive administrative principle. We have also learned something of the nature of these dispensations, of the characteristics that make them recognisable as dispensations. These truths will raise another question in the enquiring mind. We have noted the presence of dispensations, but what of their purpose? Why has it pleased God to design history in this way?

Attempting to answer questions about Divine purpose requires humility. God has confided something of His plan to us, but we should never assume that we have all the answers. Apart from revelation, God's judgements are unsearchable, 'His ways past finding out' (Rom. 11:33). We should also remember that, strictly speaking, God has only one purpose. Nonetheless, this one great overarching scheme includes within it a multitude of strands, which work, in all their diversity towards the accomplishment of God's purpose. 'His rich designs most carefully are woven, there are, with Him, no loose or broken ends.'[*] He 'worketh all things after the counsel of His own will' (Eph. 1:11).

With these caveats firmly in mind, we can recognise two important purposes in the dispensations. God has designed the ages to teach us and to test us.

Teaching

As anyone who has stood at the front of a classroom or lecture hall could confirm, no educational expert has ever produced a better definition of the process of teaching than that provided in Isaiah 28:10:

> For precept must be upon precept, precept upon precept; line upon line, line upon line; here a little, and there a little.

The prophet identifies two facts about education that any teacher ignores at his or her peril: teaching is gradual, and it is incremental. It would be pointless to expect pupils to appreciate the magnificence of Shakespeare's language until they had learned to recognise the letters of the alphabet, to read words and sentences. Similarly, there is no hope of children appreciating the logic and beauty of abstract mathematics before they have learned to add, subtract, multiply, and divide.

What is true of the individual school child is true too of the human race. We too need to learn 'precept upon precept, line upon line'. And God, in His grace, has condescended to our limitations and has, in the dispensations, provided us with a gradual and progressive revelation that leads us step by step in understanding the character and purpose of God. We

---

[*] Winifred A. Iverson, 'The Lord will perfect that which doth concern me', *Believers Hymn Book*, No. 453.

have already noted that God spoke 'at sundry times and in divers manners' (Heb. 1:1) and that this partial revelation built towards 'these last days' when He spoke unto us 'in His Son' (Heb. 1:2). Moreover, the Apostle Peter explains that even the content of this earlier revelation could not be fully understood at the time that it was given:

> Of which salvation the prophets have enquired and searched diligently, who prophesied of the grace that should come unto you: searching what, or what manner of time the Spirit of Christ which was in them did signify, when it testified beforehand the sufferings of Christ, and the glory that should follow. Unto whom it was revealed, that not unto themselves, but unto us they did minister the things, which are now reported unto you by them that have preached the gospel unto you with the Holy Ghost sent down from heaven; which things the angels desire to look into (1 Pet. 1:10–12).

God's revelation of His person and His purpose did not happen all at once. Earlier dispensations and the revelations that they received were preparatory for those that followed. 'Precept upon precept, line upon line' He patiently instructs His people.

It is helpful to our understanding of the progressive nature of revelation to think of a specific example. The truth of penal substitution states that on the cross the Lord Jesus took the sinner's place and bore the judgement – penalty – that sin deserved. This is not a truth that can be deduced from Creation. Nor, as the reaction of the unsaved so often demonstrates, is it a doctrine that is apparent or appealing to human reason. For these reasons, no doubt, God did not reveal the truth of penal substitution all at once. Rather, throughout the dispensations, He gradually unfolded this vital truth. So, right from the first dispensation we learn that sacrifice is necessary for sin to be covered. A little later, as the dispensation of conscience unfolds, we learn that not all sacrifice is acceptable to God. In the account of Cain and Abel we learn that God has a specification for sacrifice, and that it will not do to offer stuff – a life must be taken. The idea of sacrifice and substitution develops in following dispensations. On Moriah and in Egypt we learn more of the substitutionary value of sacrifice. In the dispensation of Law, all that mankind has learned about sacrifice is consolidated and elaborated in the variety and detail of the Levitical offerings, all beautiful types of Christ. Thus when the incarnate Son of God left Jerusalem for Calvary, where He, 'His own self bare our sins in His own body on the tree' (1 Pet. 2:24), humanity had been prepared, over the past millennia, to understand something of the significance of what was taking place. Progressive revelation had unfolded gradually, line upon line, communicating truth that could never have been grasped all at once. Examples could be multiplied. Paul, for instance, described the Law as 'our schoolmaster to bring us to Christ' (Gal. 3:24) and reminded the Christians in Rome that 'whatsoever things were written aforetime were written for our learning' (Rom. 15:4). But while God has progressively unfolded much of His truth, it is the revelation of Himself that is most important. The successive dispensations all fill in our picture of God, adding new details, and throwing the focus on fresh aspects of His infinite person. So, while Adam and Eve knew much of the kindness and love of God, they knew less of His holiness and His grace. The Law abundantly revealed the righteousness of God, but never imparted a full understanding of His mercy. And we, of this dispensation, have had the crowning revelation of the character of God in the One Who is 'the express image of His person' (Heb. 1:3). Uniquely, among all the ages, we are privileged to behold 'the glory of God in the face of Jesus Christ' (2 Cor. 4:6). Through the dispensations the fulness of God's glorious person has been revealed, the very pitch and perfection of the lessons that He has unfolded 'line upon line'.

TESTING

God has used His programme for the ages to teach His people. But He also uses the dispensations to test humanity. To understand the reason for this, it is important to distinguish between investigative and demonstrative testing.

Investigative testing is designed to find something out. Many of us will have had the experience of attending the doctor because we feel unwell. Unable to account for our symptoms, the doctor orders tests. We do not know the results in advance and, depending on our symptoms, may pass the time waiting for the results in a state of trepidation. Similarly, the life of the schoolchild is punctuated by tests. Past performance, ability, and application may provide indicators of the result, but it is still unknown, and the student must wait in nervous anticipation until the results become known.

Demonstrative testing is very different to this. Some of us have watches that boast of the fact that they have been tested waterproof to a certain depth. Imagine the laboratory where these tests take place. Would you expect to see the chief engineer pacing nervously to and fro as each batch of watches is tested? Would we expect him to wait eagerly for the phone to ring with the results? Of course not. He designed the watch, created its specifications so that it would be able to pass the test. He knows his handiwork through and through, and he tests it not to see if it will pass, but to prove that it will.

This is the sort of testing to which God subjects humanity. He is not trying to discover something that He does not already know. Rather, He tests to demonstrate what He knows to be the case. Sadly, He does not test us to demonstrate that we will pass. Instead, the test of each dispensation stamps the human race with failure. Failure to obey God, failure to accomplish His will are the inevitable results of Divine testing. It matters not whether the test is conducted in the lush perfection of God's garden, or the arid emptiness of the wilderness. The results are the same whether the test is carried out under Israelite theocracy or the perfect rule of the King of kings. In every test the result is the same – human failure blots and blights each dispensation.

God's Purpose for the Ages

We have already noted that God has one great purpose, one master plan for the ages. All of His other plans and programmes are just components to this great purpose. But what is that purpose? To what end does all of history tend? What part can its failures and successes, its triumphs and its tragedies play? 1 Corinthians 15:24–28 looks on to the end of history, and reveals for us the goal towards which the purpose of God is inexorably working:

> Then cometh the end, when He shall have delivered up the kingdom to God, even the Father; when He shall have put down all rule and all authority and power. For He must reign, till He hath put all enemies under His feet. The last enemy that shall be destroyed is death. For He hath put all things under his feet. But when He saith all things are put under Him, it is manifest that He is excepted, which did put all things under Him. And when all things shall

be subdued unto Him, then shall the Son also Himself be subject unto Him that put all things under Him, that God may be all in all.

God's ultimate aim is the manifestation and magnification of His glory. Insofar as glory speaks of intrinsic worth, God's glory is infinite and cannot be increased. But if glory has implicit in it the thought of intrinsic worth, it also contains the idea of the display and demonstration of that worth. All of the components of God's purpose work together to this end. 'The heavens declare the glory of God' (Ps. 19:1) and all of the material Creation is, in John Calvin's phrase, a 'most glorious theatre'.* The plan of redemption is, even in isolation, a majestic progamme – so grand that some have suggested that in it we find God's ultimate purpose. And yet, Ephesians 1:3–6 teaches us that election and salvation are not ends in themselves but fit into this greater overarching purpose:

> Blessed be the God and Father of our Lord Jesus Christ, Who hath blessed us with all spiritual blessings in heavenly places in Christ: according as He hath chosen us in Him before the foundation of the world, that we should be holy and without blame before Him in love: having predestinated us unto the adoption of children by Jesus Christ to Himself, according to the good pleasure of His will, to the praise of the glory of His grace, wherein He hath made us accepted in the beloved.

The same point is reiterated twice in the following verses of the chapter:

---

* John Calvin, *Institutes of the Christian Religion*, ed. John T. McNeill, trans. and indexed by Ford Lewis Battles (Philadelphia, PA: The Westminster Press, 1967), 1:6:2 (72)

> In Whom also we have obtained an inheritance, being predestinated according to the purpose of Him who worketh all things after the counsel of His own will: that we should be to the praise of His glory, who first trusted in Christ. In Whom ye also trusted, after that ye heard the word of truth, the gospel of your salvation: in whom also after that ye believed, ye were sealed with that holy Spirit of promise, which is the earnest of our inheritance until the redemption of the purchased possession, unto the praise of his glory (vv. 11–14).

But Ephesians chapter 1 does more than reveal that the manifestation of God's glory is His great purpose. In addition, it links that manifestation closely with God's programme for the ages. The temporal Creation, as well as the spatial, redounds with the glory of God, and the carefully planned progression of the dispensations works, as all things must, to the glory of the God Who planned them.

How, specifically, do the dispensations serve to further the glory of God? It would, perhaps, be impossible exhaustively to answer that question. However, we can readily see two ways in which He is glorified by the dispensations. Firstly, the scale and perfection of the plan reveals the greatness of the Planner. In the Divine plan for history we find two great abilities united – the power to plan and the power to execute. The poet famously – and correctly – drew a solemn lesson from a mouse:

> *But, Mousie, thou art no thy lane,*
> *In proving foresight may be vain;*
> *The best-laid schemes o' mice an' men*
> *Gang aft agley,*

> An' lea'e us nought but grief an' pain,
> For promis'd joy!
> (Robbie Burns)

Even the most meticulously planned of human programmes 'gang agley', derailed by human weakness, imperfect calculation, or unforeseeable circumstance. It is not so with our God. Though the programme, from a human perspective, seems, at times, perilously close to failure, in reality, every contingency has been foreseen, every crisis anticipated and provided for. Not only so, but the very moments that seemed to be victories for the adversary are used by God to demonstrate again and again that He is God and 'there is none else' (Isa. 45:5).

The repeated record of human failure in every dispensation also serves to magnify God's glory. In His grace, He will take the fallen and flawed sons of Adam, and transform them into the likeness of the Son of His love. All of Creation will wonder to see what heights of perfection have been achieved with such unpromising material. In each dispensation, humanity has demonstrated that it cannot claim any glory for the effects of God's work – it is, it must be, all of Him.

We must not miss this as we consider the course of the dispensations. Designed by God to teach and to test humanity, they share with every work of His hand the property of manifesting His glory. As we catch a glimpse of the hand that guided and hear the beating of the heart that planned may we echo the words of the Apostle:

> Now to him that is of power to stablish you according to my gospel, and the preaching of Jesus Christ, according to the revelation of the mystery, which was kept secret since the world began, but now is made manifest, and by the Scriptures of the prophets, according to the commandment of the

everlasting God, made known to all nations for the obedience of faith: To God only wise, be glory through Jesus Christ for ever. Amen (Rom. 16:25–27).

CHAPTER 5

CONTINUITY IN THE DISPENSATIONS

CRITICS OF DISPENSATIONALISM often allege that it is a way of interpreting the Bible that is obsessed with discontinuity, that is taken up with dividing and subdividing the Word of God. There is some truth in this allegation – dispensationalists certainly recognise differences in God's ways of dealing with mankind throughout history. But these divisions and differences are there in Scripture. It would be a very obtuse student of God's Word who failed to recognise that the world of Eden was very different from that of Israel, and the world of the Jew under the Law is just as different from that of believers during this, the Church age. Notwithstanding this, it would be a mistake to disregard the fact that the history of God's dealings with mankind is marked by both continuities and discontinuities. In this chapter we will consider some of the most important continuities in the Divine dispensations.

Mathematicians and physicists often speak of constants. These are numbers that do not change. Their value is always known, always the same. In their unchanging constancy they allow us to make sense of the universe. If they changed – just slightly, just once – then the universe would cease to be ordered and stable, and would become random and chaotic. The greatest constant is not a figure or a fraction, it is not a number at all. The greatest constant is God's character.

GOD'S CHARACTER

As human beings we are immersed in time. We are caught up in its flow and flux. Our lives are made up of change – circumstances and events flicker all about us. Our bodies, too, are involved in constant change, as cells divide and die, as we develop and then deteriorate. And, amidst all this change, we change. You are not the same person that you were last year, and you will never again be the same person – physically, mentally, or emotionally – as you are at this moment.

Change is part of our lives. But we have a God Who cannot change. He stands outside of the time that He created. He is not affected by its changes and vicissitudes. He is immutable. This immutability, this changelessness, is not just an interesting fact about God, it is a vital truth that is crucial to our understanding of history. Just as the existence of physical constants underpins our understanding of the created universe, so the fact that God's character does not change underpins our understanding of moral and redemptive history.

God's words to Israel, through Malachi, make clear both His changelessness and its implications:

> For I am the Lord, I change not; therefore ye sons of Jacob are not consumed (Mal. 3:6).

God's people had no difficult task to understand what God was like, and what He required of His people. Nor did they have to speculate about His ability or willingness to punish disobedience. They were dealing with an unchanging and unchangeable God, and their understanding of this truth was to touch every aspect of their lives.

When we look at the dispensations, it is essential that we keep the changelessness of God before us. The dispensations each emphasise different aspects of God's character, but that character remains unchanged throughout. And we should not overstate the extent to which God manifests distinct aspects of His character. In every dispensation, for example, He has revealed Himself to be righteous. In every dispensation, He has revealed Himself to be great and good. And, while the present dispensation is the dispensation of grace, and displays that attribute of God in a very special way, it would be a grave misunderstanding of Scripture to suggest that He never displayed grace in any other dispensation.

In each dispensation, God reveals more of Himself. He leads His people into an ever greater and ever deeper appreciation of the infinite and immutable being of our changeless and eternal God.

God's Principles

God's character does not change. As His principles express that character, it follows that God's principles also do not change, that they remain constant through the dispensations. Again, it is true to say that different dispensations emphasise different principles, but it is important not to overstate this difference. There are principles that remain constant throughout all of history. So, for example, sin is always sin, evil is always evil, and good is always good. Repeatedly, throughout Scripture, God has stern warnings for those who try to blur or to eradicate these unchanging moral categories. Our society constantly claims that there are no moral absolutes, that categories like good and evil are relative, even arbitrary. But God has principles that do not change, and evil remains evil, good remains good.

If the principle of sin is unchanging, so to is the principle of punishment for that sin. Ezekiel 18:20 declares 'The soul that sinneth, it shall die', and Scripture reiterates the principle that sin brings death:

> Wherefore, as by one man sin entered into the world, and death by sin; and so death passed upon all men, for that all have sinned (Rom. 5:12).

Equally clear throughout Scripture is the principle that sin brings judgement. Romans 6:23 articulates this principle:

> For the wages of sin is death; but the gift of God is eternal life through Jesus Christ our Lord.

And, in every dispensation, from Eden onwards, it has been clearly evident that God judges sin, that judgement is the inevitable and unavoidable consequence of human failure.

The principles of sin and judgement are continuous throughout the dispensations. But it is a measure of the grace and goodness of God that the principle of sacrifice also runs like a scarlet thread through the ages. The first blood shed on earth was shed to provide a covering for sinners, and from that point forward, blood was essential for the putting away of sin and the establishment of communion with God. It is telling that, in Exodus 20:24, the giving of the Law is followed immediately by instructions for the construction of an altar and the offering of sacrifice. In Leviticus 17:11, the Israelites learned of God's grace in providing for sacrifice and of the absolute necessity for blood to be shed if sin was to be taken away:

> For the life of the flesh is in the blood: and I have given it to you upon the altar to make an atonement

for your souls: for it is the blood that maketh an atonement for the soul.

The writer to the Hebrews, looking back over the Levitical order of sacrifice, summarised its guiding principle:

> And almost all things are by the law purged with blood; and without shedding of blood is no remission (Heb. 9:22).

Under the Law, then, forgiveness of sin was only possible on the basis of shed blood. And, as the writer to the Hebrews demonstrates, the shedding of blood has lost none of its importance in this dispensation of grace:

> Neither by the blood of goats and calves, but by His own blood He entered in once into the holy place, having obtained eternal redemption for us. For if the blood of bulls and of goats, and the ashes of an heifer sprinkling the unclean, sanctifieth to the purifying of the flesh: how much more shall the blood of Christ, who through the eternal Spirit offered Himself without spot to God, purge your conscience from dead works to serve the living God? (Heb. 9:12–14).

While the order and the type of sacrifice changes throughout the ages, the principle of sacrifice and the necessity for the blood of an innocent substitutionary victim to be shed remain constant as the only means by which man can approach to God. But sacrifice by itself is not sufficient. Again we look to the epistle to the Hebrews, where we get a Divinely-inspired commentary on the very first sacrifice in Scripture to be offered by man:

> By faith Abel offered unto God a more excellent sacrifice than Cain, by which he obtained witness

that he was righteous, God testifying of his gifts: and by it he being dead yet speaketh (Heb. 11:4).

As Hebrews 11 demonstrates, the principle of faith is important for every dispensation. The writer is unequivocal in his assertion that faith is an essential and fundamental requirement if we are to please God:

> But without faith it is impossible to please Him: for he that cometh to God must believe that He is, and that He is a rewarder of them that diligently seek Him (Heb. 11:6).

As the epistle to the Romans makes clear, in every dispensation, the just have lived by faith (Hab. 2:4, Rom. 1:17). The path to peace with God, the path to pleasing God always has, always will, and always must begin with faith, and continue by faith – without faith it is impossible to please Him.

GOD'S PLAN OF SALVATION

Implicit in the continuity of God's principles throughout the dispensations is another continuity, the importance of which it would be difficult to overstate. In spite of what has been suggested by some critics of dispensationalism, God's plan of salvation has not changed throughout the ages. Charles Ryrie's words are worth quoting in this connection:

> The *basis* of salvation in every age is the death of Christ; the *requirement* for salvation in every age is faith; the *object* of faith in every age is God; the *content* of faith changes in the various dispensations. It is this last point, of course, that distinguishes dispensationalism from covenant theology, but it is not a point to which the charge of teaching two ways of salvation can be attached. It

simply recognizes the obvious fact of progressive revelation.*

It is vital that we do not lose sight of the fact that salvation, in every dispensation, is possible only through the death of Christ. The sacrifices of the Old Testament – whether those offered before the giving of the Law, or those offered under the elaborate provisions of the Levitical code – had, in themselves, no power to take away sin or to save the soul: 'for it is not possible that the blood of bulls and of goats should take away sins' (Heb. 10:4). Animal sacrifices had reached their zenith under the Law. The Levitical system of offerings was complex, varied, and impressive, yet, for all that, it had no intrinsic power at all:

> For the law having a shadow of good things to come, and not the very image of the things, can never with those sacrifices which they offered year by year continually make the comers thereunto perfect (Heb. 10:1).

The animal sacrifices of the Old Testament then were pointers and tokens. Their value and efficacy came not from themselves, but from the death of Christ, which they anticipated and illustrated. Every offering of an animal, from Abel onwards, anticipated the day when the incarnate Son of God would be nailed to Calvary's cross, to 'offer Himself without spot to God' (Heb. 9:14). There, he 'offered for all time a single sacrifice for sins' (Heb. 10:12, *ESV*), dealing not just with present and future sin, but also with the sins of the past:

> For all have sinned, and come short of the glory of God; being justified freely by his grace through the redemption that is in Christ Jesus: whom God

---
* Ryrie, *Dispensationalism*, (Chicago, IL: Moody Press, 2007), 115.

> hath set forth to be a propitiation through faith in His blood, to declare His righteousness for the remission of sins that are past, through the forbearance of God; To declare, I say, at this time His righteousness: that He might be just, and the justifier of him which believeth in Jesus (Rom. 3:23–26).

We will not find anything in Scripture to suggest that there is any basis for salvation other than the death of Christ. That death dealt with sin in every age. We rejoice in the sufficiency of Christ's death to meet our own personal need. Let us not lose sight of the glorious fact that His death was sufficient not to meet our need alone, but the need of every sinner, in every age. Individuals from every dispensation will enjoy eternal blessing because of Christ's work, just as much as you or I.

> *Not all the blood of beasts*
> *On Jewish altars slain*
> *Could give the guilty conscience peace*
> *Or wash away the stain.*
>
> *But Christ, the heavenly Lamb,*
> *Takes all our sins away;*
> *A sacrifice of nobler name*
> *And richer blood than they.*
> — Isaac Watts

God's Purpose

We have already discussed God's purpose for the dispensations in a previous chapter. Nonetheless, it is worthwhile to remind ourselves that this, too, remains constant across the dispensations. God's purpose is eternal and, though it is implemented and worked out in time, it stands outside of time and can never be thwarted or diverted. Thus it stands in stark contrast to man's purposes. The history of human purpose is one of a cycle of expectation and failure. New ideas, new knowledge, new systems of government seem to offer glorious and utopian prospects, but these are inevitably – and usually rapidly – revealed as illusory. A great deal of humanity's time is taken up with making the best of failure.

It is true that each dispensation ends in failure. But this does not mean that the dispensations are a series of plans, adopted in panic or despair in response to the failure of that which has gone before. Rather, they are the orderly elucidation and execution of God's unchanging purpose, and even human failure and human rebellion contribute to the accomplishment of His eternal and inexorable purpose.

Frail as summer's flower we flourish,
Blows the wind and it is gone;
But while mortals rise and perish
God endures unchanging on,
Praise Him, Praise Him,
Praise the High Eternal One!

Henry Francis Lyte

These continuities – in God's character, His principles, His plan of salvation, and His purpose – are not the only features that remain constant across the dispensations. They are, however, the most important, with the most profound implications. In any case, it should now be clear that we cannot see the dispensations as radically discontinuous, watertight compartments of time. The reality is more complex than that.

CHAPTER 6

CHANGE IN THE DISPENSATIONS

THE PREVIOUS CHAPTER highlighted some of the most important continuities across the dispensations. Manifestly, though, the very existence of dispensations, of differing Divine administrations, means that the dispensations are also marked by change and discontinuity. It would be impossible to comprehensively survey all of the differences between the dispensations in one chapter, and many of these differences will emerge in following chapters, as we look in detail at each of the dispensations. However, it is useful to highlight some of the more important differences between the dispensations.

GOD'S SPEAKING

The first of these differences is in God's speaking. We have already seen that God spoke 'at sundry times and in divers manners' (Heb. 1:1) and it is useful to think in a little more detail about the differences in revelation from dispensation to dispensation. In addition, it is important to note that God uses different methods of revelation even within a single dispensation.

In Eden, in the dispensation of innocence, God revealed Himself in Creation, and spoke directly with man. The fall of man broke his communion with God but, in God's grace, it did not silence revelation. Creation, though marred by sin, was still capable of proclaiming 'the glory of God' (Ps. 19:1). To the general revelation of Creation was added the general revelation of conscience – mankind's innate – though not always accurate – ability to distinguish between right and wrong. But God also continued His special revelation of Himself. In the dispensations prior to the giving of the Law, that revelation was usually given directly to man by God. So, God spoke directly to Noah (Gen. 5–9), Abraham (Gen. 12–24), Isaac (Gen. 26:2–5), and to Jacob (Gen. 32:24–30). But, as the case of Joseph – who never received a direct revelation from God – demonstrates, God also spoke in other ways. Job, whose book is amongst the earliest in Scripture, expresses something of the variety of Divine revelation:

> For God speaketh once, yea twice, ['in one way, and in two' ESV] yet man perceiveth it not. In a dream, in a vision of the night, when deep sleep falleth upon men, in slumberings upon the bed; then he openeth the ears of men, and sealeth their instruction, That he may withdraw man from his purpose, and hide pride from man (Job 33:14–17).

In general, the dispensation of promise can be said to demonstrate a shift from direct revelation by God to less direct means.

The commencement of the dispensation of Law was marked by a resumption of direct revelation – Moses had very special and very particular experiences of speaking to God face-to-face. But the dispensation that was inaugurated by the giving of the Law was to be marked by the importance of two new methods of revelation – the inspiration of God's Word, and the institution of the prophetic ministry. The recording of Scripture, beginning with the books of the Pentateuch, was not just reflective of some sort of shift in human society. Rather, it was a Divinely ordained stage in the progress of revelation. As a supplement to the ongoing Scriptural revelation, God used the prophets to declare His messages for His people. Theirs was often a ministry of warning:

> Surely the Lord GOD will do nothing, but He revealeth His secret unto His servants the prophets. The lion hath roared, who will not fear? The Lord GOD hath spoken, who can but prophesy? (Amos 3:7–8).

The prophetic warnings were given so that Israel might heed them and be saved from coming judgement but, all too often, their warnings were disregarded:

> And the LORD God of their fathers sent to them by His messengers, rising up betimes, and sending; because He had compassion on His people, and on His dwelling place: but they mocked the messengers of God, and despised His words, and misused His prophets, until the wrath of the LORD arose against His people, till there was no remedy (2 Chron. 36:15–16).

Later on, the Lord Jesus was to lament, in tones of indescribable woe, the way in which Jerusalem had killed the prophets and stoned those that were sent to her (Lk. 13:34).

All of Old Testament revelation was preparatory for the event that took place 'at the end of these days', when God spoke 'unto us by His Son' (Heb. 1:1–2, *Darby*). The Apostle John, in one of the many parallels between the opening of his Gospel and the first chapter of Hebrews, describes the same event:

> And the Word was made flesh, and dwelt among us, (and we beheld his glory, the glory as of the only begotten of the Father,) full of grace and truth (Jn 1:14).

This revelation of the Father, in the Incarnate Word, was utterly unique in its medium. It was unique, too, in its content. John the Baptist, the last and the greatest of the Old Testament prophets, brought two dispensations together in pointed juxtaposition when he bore witness of the character of the Christ:

> This was he of whom I spake, He that cometh after me is preferred before me: for he was before me. And of his fulness have all we received, and grace for grace. For the law was given by Moses, but grace and truth came by Jesus Christ. No man hath seen God at any time, the only begotten Son, which is in the bosom of the Father, he hath declared him (Jn 1:15–18).

There was no incompatibility between the revelations given in each of these dispensations. After all, Isaiah had prophesied of Jehovah's Servant that 'He will magnify the law, and make it honourable' (Isa. 42:21), and the Lord Jesus Christ Himself warned His listeners 'Think not that I am come to destroy the law, or the prophets: I am not come to destroy, but to fulfil' (Mt. 5:17). In Christ God revealed nothing that was incompatible with the Law, but He revealed much that went far beyond anything that Moses or the prophets or any of the inspired writers had understood or recorded.

This unparalleled revelation of God is of crucial importance to the present dispensation. Paul emphasises this, writing to the Ephesian believers of their place in the Church, in the great structure that God is constructing in this dispensation of grace:

> Now therefore ye are no more strangers and foreigners, but fellow citizens with the saints, and of the household of God; and are built upon the foundation of the apostles and prophets, Jesus Christ Himself being the chief corner stone; in Whom all the building fitly framed together groweth unto a holy temple in the Lord: in Whom ye also are builded together for a habitation of God through the Spirit (Eph. 2:19–22).

'Jesus Christ Himself' is the key component of the revelation of God in the dispensation of grace. Also vital is 'the foundation of the apostles and prophets'.

The ministry of the apostles and prophets was essential to the laying of the Church's foundation. Their ministry, however, was limited to the laying of that foundation, and it is essential that we understand that, in the maturity of this dispensation, God does not speak, as He did in past ages, in dreams, in visions, or directly through prophetic revelation. He has given us His Word, complete in all its majestic sufficiency. Thus, in one of the earliest of the New Testament epistles, Paul anticipated the completion of the Scriptural canon and the consequent cessation of prophetic utterance:

> Charity never faileth: but whether there be prophecies, they shall fail; whether there be tongues, they shall cease; whether there be knowledge, it shall vanish away. For we know in part, and we prophesy in part. But when that which is perfect is come, then that which is in part shall be done away (1 Cor. 13:8–10).

It is important to grasp Paul's understanding of the privilege that we enjoy in this dispensation. In all previous ages, man has seen 'through a glass darkly', with a knowledge that was partial and imperfect. We have received something greater than that – the perfect, complete revelation of God in His Word. Let us never feel that, when it comes to revelation, we have something second-rate. Let us never hunger after the excitement and spectacle of prophecy, as though it somehow surpassed the Book that we hold in our hands. Let us rather rejoice in the iron-clad, leather-bound security and sufficiency of the Scriptures, 'given by inspiration of God, and profitable for doctrine, for reproof, for correction, for instruction in righteousness, that the man of God may be perfect, throughly furnished unto all good works' (2 Tim. 3:16).

Our present dispensation, then, has seen the apotheosis of Divine revelation. In the Millennium, as the believing remnant of Israel enters into the new covenant blessings that we already enjoy, they will gain a grasp and an understanding of Divine truth that will surpass anything they had previously known:

> Behold, the days come, saith the LORD, that I will make a new covenant with the house of Israel, and with the house of Judah: Not according to the covenant that I made with their fathers in the day that I took them by the hand to bring them out of the land of Egypt; which My covenant they brake, although I was an husband unto them, saith the LORD: But this shall be the covenant that I will make with the house of Israel; After those days, saith the LORD, I will put My law in their inward parts, and write it in their hearts; and will be their God, and they shall be My people. And they shall teach no more every man his neighbour, and every man his brother, saying, Know the LORD: for they shall all know Me, from the least of them unto the greatest of them, saith the LORD: for I will forgive their

iniquity, and I will remember their sin no more (Jer. 31:31–34).

The history of revelation is a vast and a vital subject, and we have scope here to do nothing more than to scratch its surface. In later chapters we will look in further detail at the way in which God provided a special revelation to each dispensation. It is, however, useful to attempt to grasp a synoptic view of the way in which our God has, through the ages, unfurled the great scroll of revelation, manifesting the glory of His person and the greatness of His purpose to His wondering and worshipping people.

God's Spirit

Chapters 13 to 17 of John's gospel are among the best-loved passages of Scripture. This is not difficult to understand. The warmth and intimacy of the moments spent by the Saviour with His own so shortly before His passion must be very precious to any believer. But it is not just the atmosphere of this passage that gives it its value. More precious still is the wealth of truth that the Lord expounded to the disciples.

His words were designed to meet the need of the disciples at a number of levels. The Lord Jesus spoke to men who would shortly be bereaved, whose faith would be shaken to its foundations. For that need He had words of comfort – 'let not your heart be troubled, neither let it be afraid' (Jn 14:27). Nor was this the empty platitude that it would have been on the lips of a mere man. The Saviour's words of comfort were backed by His promises, His prayers, and His preserving power. How the disciples must have appreciated His words and the reality of which they spoke in the days that followed, and how precious they have proven to generations of bereaved and beleaguered believers ever since.

But the Saviour was not just speaking to His sorrowing friends. He was also speaking to His servants. The disciples were men on the cusp of a new dispensation. Soon, as apostles, they would be responsible to 'go ... into all the world and preach the gospel to every creature' (Mk 16:15). And so it is that the Lord is concerned, not just to address their immediate fears, but to outline to them the character of the work that would be theirs – and ours – in the dispensation of grace. Thus, He spoke of the resources that would enable and empower their testimony for Him.

In this context, it comes as no surprise that the Saviour spoke of Scripture – to His disciples, whom He instructed 'if ye love me, keep my commandments' (Jn 14:15), and to His Father when He prayed 'sanctify them through Thy truth, Thy word is truth' (Jn 17:17). But as well as Scripture, He spoke of His Spirit:

> And I will pray the Father and He shall give you another Comforter, that He may abide with you for ever; even the Spirit of Truth; whom the world cannot receive, because it seeth Him not, neither knoweth Him, but ye know Him; for He dwelleth with you, and shall be in you (Jn 14:16–17).

It is an interesting – though ultimately speculative – exercise to try to imagine the thoughts of the disciples in response to this promise. After all, they were familiar with Old Testament Scriptures that had a great deal to say about the power and work of the Spirit of God. They could have thought of Creation, when 'the Spirit of God moved upon the face of the deep' (Gen. 1:2). As the Saviour spoke of the Spirit's ministry in reproving 'the world of sin, of righteousness, and of judgement' their minds would surely have turned to the antediluvian world, and to God's solemn word, 'My Spirit will not always strive with man' (Gen. 6:3). They could scarcely have failed to remember Joshua, Othniel, Samson, and so many other great figures of the Old Testament whose lives were marked by the presence and the power of the Holy Spirit. Why then, seeing that the Holy Spirit had been active throughout history, was the Saviour praying the Father to give the Spirit?

If they were listening carefully to the Lord they would have had their question answered by the closing clauses of v. 17: 'He dwelleth with you, and shall be in you'. In those few words, the Lord brought into focus one of the great changes introduced in the dispensation of grace.

In earlier dispensations, the Spirit had been with God's people. We read of the Spirit coming upon particular individuals at particular times. The Hebrew expression most often used to describe this event has the idea of the putting on of a garment.* It clearly implies something external and temporary – the Spirit 'with' men. A new dispensation would bring a radical change. The day of Pentecost would inaugurate this indwelling of God's Spirit, but some of the distinctive characteristics of this indwelling are outlined in these chapters. In the coming age, the Holy Spirit would not just be 'with' God's people, but He would dwell 'in' them.

This indwelling of the Spirit in the dispensation of grace would be permanent. In earlier dispensations, the operation of the Spirit in the life of the individual was temporary, even sporadic, and was linked to their empowerment for a particular undertaking or communication. So, for example, we read of Samson that 'the Spirit of the Lord began to move him at times

---

* This word, *labash*, is used, for example, of Gideon in Judg. 6:34 and of Amasai in 1 Chron. 12:18. The same word is used in Gen. 3:21 of the garments of animal skin provided by God, in Gen. 27:16 of Rebekah's disguising of Jacob and in Exod. 28:41 of the garments of the High Priest.

in the camp of Dan' (Judg. 13:25). Later in the story of Samson's life we read of discrete, isolated incidents when the Spirit of God came upon him (Judges 14:6, 19). But the Lord Jesus was clearly promising His disciples something very different when He spoke of the Comforter Who would 'abide with you for ever' (Jn 14:16). The permanent inward dwelling of the Spirit in this dispensation stands in marked contrast to the external and temporary resting of the Spirit in past ages. So, while it was perfectly appropriate for David to pray 'take not Thy Holy Spirit from me' (Ps. 51:11), the same prayer on the lips of a believer today would betray a deficient understanding of Scripture.

The operation of the Spirit will undergo a further change towards the end of the dispensation of grace. His indwelling, which commenced at Pentecost, will come to an end so far as earth is concerned, with the Rapture. The snatching away of the Church will be the catalyst for dramatic events on earth as the restraining presence of the Spirit of God is removed. The mystery of iniquity that has been heretofore withheld will have free rein. This is not to say that God's Spirit will not be active on earth during the Tribulation. Rather He will return to His Old Testament pattern of operation, coming upon individuals for particular purposes. The two witnesses, spoken of in Revelation 11 as 'two olive trees and two lampstands' (v.4) are the clearest example of this. In this connection, it is significant that references to the Spirit in Revelation are so strikingly rare, particularly in the sections of the book, from chapter 6 onwards, which describe events that are yet to be, the events of the Tribulation.

By contrast, Scripture has much to say about the operation of the Holy Spirit during the Millennium. The words of Joel 2, quoted by Peter on the day of Pentecost, still await their complete fulfilment:

> And it shall come to pass afterward, that I will pour out My spirit upon all flesh; and your sons and your daughters shall prophesy, your old men shall dream dreams, your young men shall see visions: and also upon the servants and upon the handmaids in those days will I pour out My spirit (Joel 2:28–29).

This event will be only the beginning. Among the blessings promised to Israel by the prophet Ezekiel was the indwelling of the Holy Spirit:

> Therefore say unto the house of Israel, thus saith the Lord GOD ... I will take you from among the heathen, and gather you out of all countries, and will bring you into your own land. Then will I sprinkle clean water upon you, and ye shall be clean: from all your filthiness, and from all your idols, will I cleanse you. A new heart also will I give you, and a new spirit will I put within you: and I will take away the stony heart out of your flesh, and I will give you an heart of flesh. And I will put My spirit within you, and cause you to walk in My statutes, and ye shall keep My judgments, and do them. And ye shall dwell in the land that I gave to your fathers; and ye shall be My people, and I will be your God (Ezek. 36:22–28).

And this promise was repeated and reinforced with the aid of a most vivid object lesson in the following chapter of Ezekiel, as the prophet was taken to the valley of dry bones. As Ezekiel prophesied to the bones they were reintegrated and restored and raised. All of this illustrated the power of God to accomplish His promise to His people:

> Therefore prophesy and say unto them, Thus saith the Lord GOD; Behold, O my people, I will open your graves, and cause you to come up out

> of your graves, and bring you into the land of Israel. And ye shall know that I am the LORD when I have opened your graves, O My people, and brought you up out of your graves, And shall put My spirit in you, and ye shall live, and I shall place you in your own land: then shall ye know that I the LORD have spoken it, and performed it, saith the LORD (Ezek. 37:12–14).

Throughout Scripture, from its opening to its closing chapter, the Spirit of God is active. It is only by His power and in His energy that God is served. In every dispensation, He has been central to the accomplishment of the will of God. But His operations have not been unchanging. Rather, different dispensations have and will witness differences in the way in which He works. To understand the differences that have been sketched here is vital to understanding the truth of Scripture with respect to the Spirit of God. Moreover, it is vital to understanding the truth of Scripture with respect to the dispensations.

God's Service

In every dispensation God has expected – and required – His people to serve Him. Even before the Fall, man was not simply abandoned to the otiose enjoyment of a perfect Creation – God had service for him to perform. Very generally, the service that God requires has two aspects: worship and work. The character of this service has not changed through the ages, and the words of Micah still make an excellent manifesto for the life of the believer in this dispensation:

> He hath shewed thee, O man, what is good; and what doth the LORD require of thee, but to do justly, and to love mercy, and to walk humbly with thy God? (Mic. 6:8)

At the same time, it is clear that the nature of service for God has changed with the dispensations. The responsibilities of Adam and Eve in Eden were entirely different to those of a priest in the Temple or of a believer today. Such change reflects the character of each dispensation. The distinctive responsibilities of each dispensation require a different emphasis in God's service.

The dispensational change in the service of God can be seen especially in relation to His worship. While we read of worship first in connection with Abraham in Genesis 18:2 (translated as 'bowed himself'), the sacrifices that were offered from Abel onwards all indicate the desire of man to worship God, and the acceptance of man's worship by God. As we follow the pathway of the patriarchs through Scripture, we encounter altar after altar, and sacrifice after sacrifice, every one redolent of the worship of these men of God.

In the dispensation of Law, Divine service was elaborated and codified in Israel's ceremonial Law. In the book of Leviticus, we have a manual for the worship of God under the Law. We cannot but marvel at its richness and complexity, and we do well to profit from the lessons that it has for us concerning the character and work of Christ, and the requirements for our approach to Him.

Today, however, we do not make our way up to Jerusalem, to worship God at the Temple. We no longer have to find animal sacrifices to bring to Him. In this dispensation, the service of God has undergone a radical paradigm shift. This shift was foretold by the Lord Jesus Christ as He spoke to the Samaritan woman. Resisting her attempts to sidetrack the conversation into religious and nationalistic debate, He told her of an imminent alteration in the worship of God:

> Woman, believe me, the hour cometh, when ye shall neither in this mountain, nor yet at Jerusalem, worship the Father. Ye worship ye know not what: we know what we worship: for salvation is of the Jews. But the hour cometh, and now is, when the true worshippers shall worship the Father in spirit and in truth: for the Father seeketh such to worship Him. God is a Spirit: and they that worship Him must worship him in spirit and in truth (Jn 4:21–24).

In contrast to the Temple-based worship of an earlier dispensation, worship in the dispensation of grace is not limited by location or circumscribed by ethnic constraints. God still desires the worship of His people, but it is worship 'in spirit and in truth' that brings gladness to His heart.

This is no academic point. Rather, a grasp of the dispensational change in the service of God has immense practical impact on our public worship. Christendom in general has pilfered its forms of worship from an earlier dispensation. It has adopted its priestly class, its physical 'places of worship', its musical instruments, its incense, and its pomp. What a contrast to all this is the simplicity of the spiritual worship that God seeks in this dispensation. May we seek to ensure that, in our individual lives and in our public gatherings, He does not seek for it in vain.

This chapter does not attempt to provide an exhaustive list of the differences between the dispensations. However, the differences that have been outlined are amongst the most significant and understanding them will assist us greatly in grasping the distinctiveness of the dispensations, and in better appreciating the dispensational features that apply particularly to us in this the day of grace.

CHAPTER 7

THE DISPENSATION OF INNOCENCE

'A GARDEN', THE POET remarked, 'is a lovesome thing.'* He could scarcely have uttered a less controversial sentiment. Even the most horticulturally inept of us find pleasure in the beauty of a well-tended garden. We admire not just the intricate beauty of Creation, but the skill, taste and ingenuity of its designer. Even at their best, the gardens that we enjoy are imperfect. Death and disorder are always waiting to take control, and can only be held at bay by the unrelenting vigilance and constant hard work of the dedicated gardener.

It is always thus in our world. We are often moved as we contemplate the beauty and variety of the natural world. But, even in our moments of delight, we can never quite lose sight of the fact that we look at a damaged masterpiece, a broken sculpture, and a slashed canvas. Creation 'groans and travails' (Rom. 8:22) and our ears ever catch the strain of its still sad music.

It was not always so. Once Creation glistered pristine from the hand of God, Who looked upon it, and pronounced it 'very good' (Gen. 1:31). Once, 'the

---

* Thomas Edward Brown, 'My Garden' in T.E. Brown, *Old John and Other Poems*, (London: Macmillan and Co, 1893), 177.

morning stars sang together and all the sons of God shouted for joy' (Job 38:7) as their privileged eyes encompassed the majesty of Divine handiwork. How they must have wondered and worshipped as they surveyed the variety of Creation, as they saw the character of the God that they served made evident in a four-dimensional universe. Small wonder that they shouted, drawing each other's attention to this detail and that, to each curious form, each cunningly-wrought being.

And in all of that universe, they surely found no beauty to compare with the garden planted by God 'eastwards in Eden' (Gen. 2:8). Here perfection was piled on perfection. An unfallen Creation, void of disorder, was ordered by the hand of God into a verdant and varied paradise, the dwelling place of Creation's honoured head. We cannot imagine what sights greeted Adam's opening eyes, the sounds that filled the ears that were lately dust, the smells that filled the nostrils still warm from the breath of God.

But all of this wonder and all of this glory are as nothing to what took place in the garden. Just as the most exquisite golden mounting is rendered insignificant by the beauty of the jewel that it bears, so the event for which Eden provided the setting relegated all of its glory to the background. Here it was that God spoke to Adam, that the Creator revealed Himself to His Creation. And here it was that the very first of the dispensations was inaugurated.

Every dispensation is distinct in its character and content from every other age. Yet it is true to say that, in a number of very special ways, this first of earth's ages is unique. It is unique in its setting. None of the other dispensations unfolded or will unfold in a sinless world. Even though the Millennium will see the reversal of much of sin's baleful effect, those thousand glorious years will still pass in a world that has been marked by the Fall. The dispensation of innocence is unique, too, in the characters that people it. Here, alone, do we see mankind in its pristine state, devoid of any trace or effect of sin. But, beyond all this, the dispensation of innocence is unique in its tragedy. Every dispensation involves failure and, thus, inescapably, every dispensation involves tragedy. But none is quite as tragic as this. The dispensation opens with perfect man in the garden, and closes with fallen man, cast out from Eden's perfection. It begins with man walking with God, and enjoying communion with Him, and ends with him scurrying shamefaced, seeking ineffectual refuge amongst the trees that God had provided for the blessing of man. The dispensation opens with the angels' song; it closes with the angels' sword. And yet, with all its tragedy and loss, the dispensation is not without its glimmers – faint and distant though they be – of future triumph, restoration, and glory.

REVELATION

It is characteristic of the revelations that commence each of the dispensations that they allow little room for misinterpretation. God does not require mankind to grope in a fog of uncertainty. When He places responsibilities upon humanity He makes the nature of those responsibilities very clear. Thus it is that men and women can never plead ignorance in extenuation of their disobedience. Their failure is not a failure to know, but to do.

The first of the dispensational revelations exemplifies this very clearly. God's command to Adam was not a complex one. It was delivered with absolute clarity. And, capturing God's goodness and His righteousness, it blended the positive with the negative:

> And the LORD God took the man, and put him into the garden of Eden to dress it and to keep it. And the LORD GOD commanded the man, saying, Of every tree of the garden thou mayest freely eat: But of the tree of the knowledge of good and evil, thou shalt not eat of it: for in the day that thou eatest thereof thou shalt surely die (Gen. 2:16–17).

It is significant that, as v. 18 makes clear, this revelation was given to Adam alone. Adam was not just the head of his wife – though he was that too. Rather, he stood before God as the responsible head of humanity, the federal head of the race and as its sole representative he received the Divine command. It was his responsibility not only to obey that command, but to declare it too. This he did, but the garbled account of that command quoted to the serpent by Eve raises the possibility that the communication of the Divine decree had not been entirely accurate.

In this way, Adam stands as a stark warning to all those who have been entrusted with Divine revelation. With that revelation comes a responsibility to publish it, and the warning given by God to Ezekiel should weigh heavily upon all those who, through grace, have come to a knowledge of the truth of God's Word:

> When I bring the sword upon a land, if the people of the land take a man of their coasts, and set him for their watchman: if when he seeth the sword come upon the land, he blow the trumpet, and warn the people; then whosoever heareth the sound of the trumpet, and taketh not warning; if the sword come, and take him away, his blood shall be upon his own head. He heard the sound of the trumpet, and took not warning; his blood shall be upon him. But he that taketh warning shall deliver his soul. But if the watchman see the sword come, and blow not

the trumpet, and the people be not warned; if the sword come, and take any person from among them, he is taken away in his iniquity; but his blood will I require at the watchman's hand (Ezek. 33:2–6).

The Apostle Paul felt the weight of this responsibility and, as he spoke to the elders of the church at Ephesus, he declared:

Wherefore I take you to record this day, that I am pure from the blood of all men (Acts 20:26).

Could Adam have said the same? Can you?

RESPONSIBILITY

Revelation from God placed a single clear responsibility upon Adam and Eve. Of all the trees of the garden there was one – and one alone – of which they could not eat. To eat of that tree would be to die.

It is difficult for us to read the story and consider this prohibition without asking questions regarding its reason. Why did God forbid this one tree to them? Was the prohibition merely arbitrary? Why did God make the Fall possible? Could an omniscient God not have provided an environment for mankind where sin was impossible?

These questions are legitimate, but ultimately unanswerable. God's judgements are unsearchable, His ways past finding out (Rom. 11:33). In accordance with His infinite wisdom He was pleased to create a world where sin was possible. Sin was never the will of God, nor dare we ever suggest that it originated with Him. Nonetheless, in Eden, He knowingly allowed events to be set in train that would ultimately issue in the agonising sufferings and shameful death of His well beloved Son. And yet, He ordered Creation so – the death of Christ was in the mind of God from eternity, and not just from Eden. It was no contingent emergency response to unforeseen circumstances. And while we cannot explain or account for this, we rest in the certainty that God works all things to 'the glory of His grace' (Eph. 1:6). Like Job, faced with the infinities of God, we lay our hand upon our mouth (Job 40:4), and exclaim 'He hath done all things well!' (Mk 7:37).

This notwithstanding, we can say that the making of man in God's image included giving to him a free will, and man's ability freely to obey God would be meaningless in a world where disobedience was impossible. Those of us who have children are delighted by their obedience and disappointed by their disobedience but we would not, for all that, have them become mindless automatons who obeyed because they had no choice, because they could do nothing else. In view of the fact that human fatherhood is modelled on and imitative of Divine fatherhood (Eph. 3:14-15) and of the numerous Scriptures that reveal to us the delight that the Father had in the voluntary submission and obedience of His perfect Son, it seems legitimate to suggest that what God desired was the voluntary, and not the enforced, obedience of Adam and Eve.

But if the tree, and the prohibition that it entailed, was necessary for the full expression of the character of humanity, it was also requisite for the manifestation of the character of God. God is a righteous God and, in the Garden of Eden, the tree of the knowledge of good and evil was a visible, tangible manifestation of that righteousness. The whole garden proclaimed God's goodness and power but the tree was a unique and potent reminder that though great and good, God is also holy.

It was this righteous God that Adam and Eve served and the revelation that He gave to them established the nature of that service. Its terms were scarcely onerous.

God had withheld nothing that humanity required and, in Eden, they found in addition all that they could desire. But neither the clarity of the revelation or the simplicity of its requirements were sufficient to prevent humanity from rebelling against God and tumbling a whole race – and a whole Creation – headlong into tragedy.

Rebellion

The epistle to the Romans wastes no words in cutting to the heart of the dire events that took place in Eden. It was 'one man's disobedience' (Rom 5:19), a rebellion against God's will and God's word. But the detail of the events leading up to that act of disobedience will reward our careful consideration. The Fall was a prototype sin. It established the enduring pattern of Satanic stratagem and human failure, and is re-enacted in miniature again and again.

The youngest believer, if at all well taught, ought to be familiar with the three inveterate enemies of the believer – the world, the flesh, and the devil (Eph. 2:1–3). Adam and Eve, living in a perfect world and possessed of an unfallen nature, faced only one of these foes. In them Satan's desire to defile all that brought pleasure to God and to thwart the Divine purpose found its instruments. His attack upon them revealed his tactics, tactics which have, in essence, never altered. Satan, in the guise of the serpent came to the garden to unleash a three-pronged attack on Divine order, Divine ordinance, and the Divine character.

Headship was built into Creation by God. Adam, we are reminded, 'was first formed, then Eve' (1 Tim. 2:13). This order was undermined by Satan, who found in Eve an ear that would listen to his voice and a mind that was pliable to his seductive suggestions. And, as events unfolded, Eve assumed a position of headship that she should never have occupied, even as Adam abdicated the position that was creatorially his. Thus it was that Satan commenced his assault on God's purpose for humanity, and so it has continued ever since. God's statement to Eve – 'thy desire shall be to thy husband, and he shall rule over thee' (Gen. `) foretold the continuing struggle for headship that began in Eden.

It is worth pausing here, to stress the important practical fact that God expects that those whom He has saved demonstrate a scriptural understanding of headship, and not the distorted fallen perspective of the world. In our homes and in our assemblies He looks for that which He does not find anywhere else – an acknowledgement of Divine order and Divine headship. When angels see it, they are instructed and edified (1 Cor. 11:10); when God sees it, He rejoices.

Even as Satan attacked Divine order, he assaulted Divine authority. The serpent's mocking question 'Yea, hath God said...?' (Gen. 3:1) went to the heart of the matter. So much suffering could have been avoided had Eve only taken a firm stand upon the accuracy and authority of God's word. She could not have said, as the Lord Jesus Christ was to do in similar circumstances 'it is written', but she could – and should – have appealed directly to what God said. Her failure to do that was the beginning of the end – her whole defeat was wrapped up in that simple omission.

That there are lessons here for today is manifest. Satan and his serpentine servants still insinuate, still suggest, still inquire 'Yea, hath God said...?' The authority and veracity of God's Word are constantly queried and, like Eve, it needs only the tiniest retreat to inaugurate a full-scale rout. We need to learn this lesson from Eve's experience, and we need to learn it well. But Eve has another warning for us. Our reliance in times of attack must be upon what the Word of God actually says. Not on what we think it says, not on what we wish it said, but on what it does say. Re-reading the story of man's first rebellion should send us to our knees as we appreciate something of the wiliness of our foes. But it should also drive us to our desks and to our Bibles, that we might know, understand, and rely upon the Word of God.

Satan did not stop at attacking God's order and God's ordinance. As he continued his onslaught on Eve, he moved to misrepresent the character of God. Satan first called into question the righteousness of God. His belittling dismissal of the consequences of sin – 'ye shall not surely die' (Gen. 3:4) – implicitly made God a liar, and suggested that His truthfulness and trustworthiness could not be relied upon. Beyond that, he denied God's goodness. God, he suggested, was a petty despot, denying humanity the full achievement of its potential simply because of jealousy. No other reason than a fear that Adam and Eve would 'be as gods' (Gen. 3:5) underpinned His prohibition of the tree.

We may well wonder that Eve should fall for such an egregious misrepresentation of God's person. She was the daily, the constant recipient of God's goodness and grace. From His hand she received not just an ample provision, but a bewildering variety of perfection. Not a thing that she needed was left unsupplied. And yet her act demonstrated unequivocally her acceptance of Satan's twisted caricature of God.

Satan has continued to perpetuate this caricature, and many people today hold this distorted view of God. They have accepted the lie that it is possible to sin without consequence, that no serious attention need be paid to God's laws. In addition, by their words as well as by their actions, they declare that God does not have His creature's best interests at heart, but is concerned only to limit their development and hamper their enjoyment.

Salvation has brought to us the knowledge of 'the only true God, and Jesus Christ, whom [He] hast sent' (Jn 17:3). But just as Eve, with every tangible confirmation of God's goodness, was not immune from satanic attack, so we, who have known so much of His grace, can find ourselves assaulted by false notions of God. We would never express or acknowledge these but, deep in the recesses of our heart, we become unconvinced of His righteousness, His goodness, and His love. As with Eve, such doubts will weaken us, leaving us vulnerable to Satan's stratagems. True are the words of Daniel that 'the people that do know their God shall be strong, and do exploits' (Dan. 11:32).

Faced with these attacks upon the stability of Divine order, the veracity of God's Word, and the integrity of God's character, Eve gave way on all fronts. Hook, line, and sinker, she took Satan's bait. And once the truths on which she should have stood firm had been abandoned, her moral sense changed. Before Satan's words had distorted her thinking, the tree must surely have been an object of reverential dread. Now her perceptions had changed, and she 'saw that the tree was good for food, and that it was pleasant to the eyes, and a tree to be desired to make one wise' (Gen. 3:6). And, with an inexorable inevitability, her thoughts shaped her actions, and she took of the fruit.

What of Adam in all of this? Scripture leaves no room for doubt about his guilt. 1 Timothy 2:14 reminds us that 'Adam was not deceived'. Eve was the blinded victim of a satanic scam, but Adam sinned with open eyes, and a full consciousness of what he did. Thus, Romans 5:19 speaks of 'one man's disobedience'. Adam placed his love for Eve and his desire to continue to enjoy her company above his love for, and loyalty to God. And so humanity's federal head, who had been placed by God in such a prominent position, and 'crowned with glory and honour' (Heb. 2:7), deliberately and reflectively rebelled against the God Who made him and, by one act of disobedience, occasioned fearful results for himself, the human race, and for all of Creation.

RETRIBUTION

It is no exaggeration to say that the results of the Fall were cataclysmic for humanity and for the cosmos. What must be stressed, however, is that God's judgement on man's sin is not the wreaking of a wanton and disproportionate vengeance. The retribution that God imposed upon His Creation was a vindication of that very righteousness that Satan had denied and Eve had doubted. Moreover, even in its severity, the promise of a redeemer given by God – the 'Protoevangelium' or 'first gospel' – demonstrated that God was gracious as well as just. Thus, though God's justice was righteous in its severity, and comprehensive in its scope, it did not consign humanity to the hopeless despair that its sin merited. Habakkuk's great prayer 'in wrath remember mercy' (3:2) was the cry of a man who had heard the report of God and His work, and knew that his request was in accordance with the character and the conduct of God. The implications of God's judgement of Adam's sin would easily fill a volume, but it is useful briefly to consider the most significant effects of this first dispensational judgement.

Romans 5:12 is stark and uncompromising in its statement of the results of Adam's disobedience:

> Wherefore, as by one man sin entered into the world, and death by sin; and so death passed upon all men, for that all have sinned.

The extent to which animal and plant death was a part of Creation before the Fall has been the subject of much debate. Whatever position we adopt on this question, it is clear that human death, at the very least, was not an integral part of God's Creation but came as an interloper and an invader. And that death had spiritual and physical aspects. The moment Adam sinned, he and Eve died spiritually – their newfound desire to hide from God is an eloquent testimony to their new condition. At the same moment, the inexorable process of physical death began to work in their beings, starting them on the downward incline that would end with their physical death. And that death would irresistibly 'pass upon all men', and will continue to do so until it stands alone as the last enemy and is destroyed by the victorious power of a risen Christ. For, 1 Corinthians 15 tells us:

> But now is Christ risen from the dead, and become the firstfruits of them that slept. For since by man came death, by man came also the resurrection of the dead. For as in Adam all die, even so in Christ shall all be made alive (1 Cor. 15:20–22).

Death was not the first enemy – Satan and sin claim precedence over it. But they and it will one day be destroyed as the final result of a victory so great that it has overcome all the wreck of Adam's fall.

Though Scripture does not use the term 'Fall' to describe the events that took place in Eden, it is, nonetheless, an entirely appropriate description. In Eden, natural man was at the peak of his perfection – sin hurled him down from that pinnacle, debasing and devaluing humanity. As a consequence of sin, humanity lost both its inherent and its official dignity.

Genesis 1:26 is the first mention in Scripture of man. We are allowed to eavesdrop on a conversation between Divine persons:

> And God said, Let Us make man in Our image, after Our likeness: and let them have dominion over the

fish of the sea, and over the fowl of the air, and over the cattle, and over all the earth, and over every creeping thing that creepeth upon the earth.

Man was designed by God with an inherent dignity that was unique – of all Creation, he alone was created in the image of God. Indeed, Luke 3:38 brings the genealogy of the Lord Jesus Christ to an end with 'Adam, the son of God'. That this was not a physical likeness is obvious. Mentally, morally, and socially, humanity bore the stamp of its Creator, and was fitted for a relationship with Him in a way that the lower Creation never could be. But Genesis 5 makes it clear that this image was tragically defaced by the fall:

> In the day that God created man, in the likeness of God made He him; Male and female created he them; and blessed them, and called their name Adam, in the day when they were created. And Adam lived an hundred and thirty years, and begat a son in his own likeness, and after his image; and called his name Seth (Gen. 5:1–3).

Adam was created 'in the likeness of God', but in Seth, he begot 'a son in his own likeness'. Mankind was no longer in the image of God. That is not to say that the image of God was entirely eradicated from mankind. Its traces are still to be found in the sporadic nobility and greatness of human action. It can be glimpsed in human creativity and intellect. But these, at best, are the vestigial traces of what Adam was.

Adam was given an official as well as an inherent dignity. Humanity was given dominion 'over the fish of the sea, and over the fowl of the air, and over the cattle, and over all the earth, and over every creeping thing that creepeth upon the earth'. Psalm 8 expands upon the dignity freely conferred on humanity by God:

> What is man, that thou art mindful of Him? and the son of man, that Thou visitest him? For Thou hast made him a little lower than the angels, and hast crowned him with glory and honour. Thou madest him to have dominion over the works of Thy hands; Thou hast put all things under his feet: all sheep and oxen, yea, and the beasts of the field; the fowl of the air, and the fish of the sea, and whatsoever passeth through the paths of the seas (Ps. 8:4–8).

Man's disobedience destroyed this dominion. God's words to Adam revealed that the nature of his mastery over Creation had decisively changed. No longer would Creation's resources be freely offered to meet the needs of humanity. Now, every resource would have to be wrestled from a grudging earth:

> And unto Adam he said, Because thou hast hearkened unto the voice of thy wife, and hast eaten of the tree, of which I commanded thee, saying, Thou shalt not eat of it: cursed is the ground for thy sake; in sorrow shalt thou eat of it all the days of thy life; thorns also and thistles shall it bring forth to thee; and thou shalt eat the herb of the field; in the sweat of thy face shalt thou eat bread, till thou return unto the ground; for out of it wast thou taken: for dust thou art, and unto dust shalt thou return (Gen. 3:17–19).

For all the technological advancements that the millennia have seen, this situation has not changed. Whether it be in horticulture, farming or in the extraction of minerals, man must expend enormous effort to exploit the resources of Creation. No longer the gladly acknowledged master of a compliant Creation, he must rule it as a tyrannical despot, never secure in his control, never stable in his mastery, always struggling, but never quite able, to keep the tremendous forces of Creation productively in check.

Mankind's relationship with Creation, then, was radically altered by sin. So was the relationship between man and woman. Eve, in the lovely phrase of Genesis 2:18, was a 'help meet' for Adam. She was his complement, fitted by Divine design to aid and assist her husband. As we have already noted in passing, that relationship did not escape the corrosive effects of sin. Moreover, the procreative role that was woman's great glory would now be marked by suffering and pain:

> Unto the woman he said, I will greatly multiply thy sorrow and thy conception; in sorrow thou shalt bring forth children; and thy desire shall be to thy husband, and he shall rule over thee (Gen.3:16).

Again we see the true nature of sin. Harmony is disrupted, and sorrow and suffering introduced.

Creation, too, was fundamentally altered by the consequences of Adam's sin. Romans 8 starkly presents the reality of the pervasive effects of Adam's disobedience:

> For the earnest expectation of the creature waiteth for the manifestation of the sons of God. For the creature was made subject to vanity, not willingly, but by reason of Him who hath subjected the same in hope, because the creature itself also shall be delivered from the bondage of corruption into the glorious liberty of the children of God. For we know that the whole Creation groaneth and travaileth in pain together until now (Rom. 8:19–22).

Even the most cursory glance at the natural world makes the appalling scale of this alteration obvious. God had declared that Creation was 'very good' and it still has the potential to humble and amaze us. But for all its beauty, we cannot look too long or too hard without realizing that nature is, in Tennyson's often-quoted phrase, 'red in tooth and claw'. Predation, struggle, and death are the order of the animal kingdom, for most creatures, life is short and brutal, a constant battle for survival. This is so basic a feature of Creation as we know it, that it seems impossible to conceive of a world that does not groan and travail under the bondage of corruption. But such conditions did exist – and will again. Isaiah's beautiful millennial prophecy evokes a world freed from the bondage of sin, and allows us to understand a little of the world that Adam and Eve had known:

> The wolf also shall dwell with the lamb, and the leopard shall lie down with the kid; and the calf and the young lion and the fatling together; and a little child shall lead them. And the cow and the bear shall feed; their young ones shall lie down together: and the lion shall eat straw like the ox. And the sucking child shall play on the hole of the asp, and the weaned child shall put his hand on the cockatrice' den (Isa. 11:6–8).

This was the happy harmony that sin disrupted, the idyllic bliss that disobedience destroyed.

We have traced a grim picture. We survey a battlefield on which the enemy of God and of humanity has a decisive victory. Decisive, but not final. We could not turn from the scene without glimpsing once again the single shaft of Divine sunlight that pierces the clouds. For even in his greatest victory, Satan's inevitable defeat is implicit:

> And the LORD God said unto the serpent, Because thou hast done this, thou art cursed above all cattle, and above every beast of the field; upon thy belly shalt thou go, and dust shalt thou eat all the days of

thy life: and I will put enmity between thee and the woman, and between thy seed and her seed; it shall bruise thy head, and thou shalt bruise his heel (Gen. 3:14–15).

This protoevangelical promise shines brightly in the debris of a fallen Creation, and reminds us of the unfailing goodness and greatness of God. Satan's defeat was foretold, and notwithstanding his unfailing efforts to thwart God's purpose, the moment came when the Seed of the woman, in majestic power did bruise the serpent's head, defeating 'him that hath the power of death' (Heb. 2:14) and triumphing over him in His cross (Col. 2:15). Nor, for the believer, is this the only hope to be found in the story of the Fall. We can hardly consider the catalogue of sin's consequences without thinking of the One in Whom they are reversed. So, we cannot think about the disobedience of Adam, without being reminded of the obedience of Christ. We cannot remember that 'in Adam all died' without recalling that 'in Christ shall all be made alive' (1 Cor. 15:22). We cannot contemplate the lost headship of the first Adam without thinking of the second Adam, Who, in His perfect humanity, 'was crowned with glory and honour', Who rode upon the ass's colt, Who rebuked the storm, and Who directed an argentine fish to Peter's hook. And we cannot readily think about the defacement of the Divine image without joyously realizing that we, as redeemed sinners, are even now being changed 'from glory to glory' (2 Cor. 3:18) and that 'when He shall appear, we shall be like Him for we shall see Him as He is' (1 Jn 3:2–3).

This first dispensation is replete with importance for us. It presents us with a prototype of the dispensations, and establishes not just the pattern but the principles that will shape God's dealings with mankind. It takes us from Eden to exclusion and from glory to gloom. It reveals the cunning of Satan and the weakness of humanity. It makes us sorrowful. Yet, by God's grace it cannot make us despair, for we trace in the gloom the glow of God's grace, and rejoice that His hand turns history to His eternal glory.

CHAPTER 8

THE DISPENSATION OF CONSCIENCE

LIKE THE FIRST dispensation, the the dispensation of conscience unfolded in a unique age. Its events took place in a postlapsarian world – a world after the Fall. At the same time it was an antediluvian world – a world before the Flood. As such it was marked by both similarities and dissimilarities with our own world.

The New Testament stresses both these features of this world. For Peter, it is the dissimilarities that are most significant:

> Knowing this first, that there shall come in the last days scoffers, walking after their own lusts, and saying, Where is the promise of his coming? For since the fathers fell asleep, all things continue as they were from the beginning of the Creation. For this they willingly are ignorant of, that by the word of God the heavens were of old, and the earth standing out of the water and in the water: whereby the world that then was, being overflowed with water, perished: but the heavens and the earth, which are now, by the same word are kept in store, reserved unto fire against the day of judgment and perdition of ungodly men (2 Pet. 3:3–7).

The 'world that then was' is presented as a radically different place from the present world. These scoffers err in their wilful ignorance of God's intervention in judgement upon that old world. (It is worth noting, in passing, how well the description of these scoffers fits the evolutionists of today, who base their ideas upon the theory of uniformity, the assumption that 'all things continue as they were from the beginning of the Creation'.) In fact, as Peter makes clear, things have not always been as they are – between 'the world that then was' and us there stands the momentous judgement of God, which has left its imprint upon Creation. Geologically, meteorologically, and ecologically the world today is a very different place from that which Adam and Eve entered, and in which Cain, Abel and the rest of antediluvian humanity lived.

By contrast, when the Lord Jesus Christ speaks of this world He emphasises its similarity to the world of today:

> But as the days of Noah were, so shall also the coming of the Son of man be. For as in the days that were before the Flood they were eating and drinking, marrying and giving in marriage, until the day that Noe entered into the ark, and knew not until the Flood came, and took them all away; so shall also the coming of the Son of man be (Mt. 24:37–39).

In physical terms, the world was dramatically changed. So far as the behaviour, the interests, and the complacency of its inhabitants were concerned, though, it bore a clear resemblance to the world that exists today, and that will exist immediately prior to the coming of the Son of Man.

Nor is the resemblance to our own world and society limited to those aspects highlighted by the Lord Jesus. As we look at Genesis 4–6, we can hardly escape a sense of recognition, of familiarity, for the roots of our own society are clearly to be seen in the activities and interests of the sons of Cain. We notice, for example, that this antediluvian world was marked by the building of cities. It is significant that it was Cain who built the first city (Gen. 4:17), and doubly so that he built Enoch (and called it after his son) in direct and calculated defiance of God's judgement that Cain would be 'a fugitive and a vagabond ... in the earth' (v.12). This first city, then, is built in rebellion against God, and we do not have to read too much further into Genesis to have the link between the rejection of God and the construction of cities confirmed for us. God had intended man to live in a garden. His instructions to Adam after the Fall presupposed an agrarian life. But man has resisted God's will, and in all ages has built cities and gathered men together to live in them. And in every age – and most certainly in our own – cities have been centres of sin, of vice, and of rebellion.

The world before the Flood was also marked by moral departure. In Eden, God had instituted marriage as a union between one man and one woman. Now, just six generations later, man is departing from Divinely instituted moral order. 'Lamech took unto him two wives' (v.19). And that departure would continue to develop as history unfolded. It would mar the lives of some of the greatest men of God in the Old Testament, and continues, unabated and flourishing in our own day, where the Scriptural concept of marriage is under fierce and often successful assault.

That this was a world of entertainment is indicated in the description of Jubal: 'he was the father of all such as handle the harp and organ' (v.21). Cut off from God, and cast out of His presence, man was conscious of an emptiness in his soul. And, rather than turning back to the God against Whom he had sinned, he turned instead to the beginnings of the 'entertainment industry'. Still today, the entertainment industry peddles its products to men and women who are trying to fill a void in their souls, who try to fill the God-shaped vacuum with the noxious nostrums that repackage vice and immorality as entertainment.

Furthermore, this was a world of technological advancement. Tubal-cain was 'an instructor of every artificer in brass and iron' (v.22). Even in his fallen state, humanity retains the creative ability given by God. Yet all his technological progress does not bring any real or lasting improvement, and the text of Scripture juxtaposes the technological advancements represented by Tubal-cain with the vengeful violence of Lamech, who glories in his out-caining of Cain:

> Then Lamech said to his wives: 'Adah and Zillah, hear my voice; Wives of Lamech, listen to my speech! For I have killed a man for wounding me, even a young man for hurting me. If Cain shall be avenged sevenfold, Then Lamech seventy-sevenfold.' (v.23–24, NKJV)

Beyond this juxtaposition, there is no evidence to suggest that the artifice of Tubal-cain provided Lamech with his deathly weapon. But we know from history that there is not a technological advancement that humanity has made that has not been used in violence against fellow human beings.

Finally, and perhaps most searchingly, this antediluvian world was marked by a breakdown in separation. The precise meaning of the opening verses of Genesis 6 is the subject of much discussion and debate. Regardless, however, of the exact interpretation that we give to these difficult verses, it is clear that they present the bringing together of that which God had separated. The results of this admixture went beyond that which God had purposed in Creation. Giants in Scripture speak of that which is abnormal, and Genesis 6 presents us with the freakish and deformed results of the failure of separation. This failure would manifest itself again and again in the centuries that would follow. Satan would do everything in his power to forestall his foretold doom, to corrupt the Godly line and to make impossible the coming of the Seed of the woman Who would bring about his final defeat. Thus it is that Satan ever assaults the separation of God's people. The end product of failed separation is often large and superficially impressive but, even in its impressive scale it represents the corruption and the deformation of Divine purpose and plan.

Such was the character of the world during the second dispensation. Amongst other things, it is significant for what it reveals about the character of sin. Man's departure from God after the Fall was not a gradual drift. Rather, having turned his back on God, man made full speed away from all that was of God or that was in accordance with His will. Man's soul was not slowly corroded – the contagion of sin worked a rapid and an irresistible corruption.

It would be wrong, however, simply to accentuate the negative. Conditions were undoubtedly dark. Yet we begin to see a truth that subsequent dispensations would amplify. God is always able to preserve a people for Himself. So, amidst the wholesale rebellion and departure of the world, there were those who 'called upon the name of the Lord' (Gen. 4:26). In this world there was a man who 'walked with God' (v.22) and who 'pleased God' (Heb. 11:5). In this world, too, there was a man 'who found grace in the eyes of the Lord' (Gen. 6:8), who believed and obeyed God and who 'became heir of the righteousness which is by faith' (Heb. 11:7). Thrillingly, this was also an age that witnessed the snatching up of Enoch, who 'was translated that he should not see death; and was not found, because God had translated him' (Heb. 11:5), a lovely picture of the Rapture of God's people in our present dispensation of grace.

As we sketch from Scripture the outline of this antediluvian society, let us learn the lesson that we can never make circumstances the excuse for our failure to live for God. These heroes of faith preserved their separation and their testimony in a day not much different from our own. 'Compassed about with so great a cloud of witnesses' (Heb. 12:1) can we do less?

Revelation

Scripture has surprisingly little to say about direct revelation from God during the dispensation of conscience. It is, however, clear that revelations were given that have not been recorded for us. For example, Hebrews 11 tells us that Abel offered an acceptable sacrifice to God not by luck, or by happy chance, but by faith. Faith, we know, 'cometh by hearing, and hearing by the Word of God', and so we can conclude that Abel offered a sacrifice in accordance with Divine instructions and that Cain's failure to offer a suitable sacrifice was not simply a regrettable mistake, but disobedience to the Word of God. We also know, of course, that God spoke directly to Noah towards the end of the dispensation, and that Noah became 'a preacher of righteousness', conveying God's message by his words, as well as his actions. In addition, God's words in Genesis 6:3 indicate that, during this age, His Spirit was striving with man.

These acts of special revelation, however, do not constitute the dispensational revelation, for they do not provide the basis upon which the human race would be tested. To understand the nature of that revelation we need to return to Eden. There, as Satan tempted Eve, he offered her a tantalising prospect:

> And the serpent said unto the woman, Ye shall not surely die: For God doth know that in the day ye eat thereof, then your eyes shall be opened, and ye shall be as gods, knowing good and evil. And when the woman saw that the tree was good for food, and that it was pleasant to the eyes, and a tree to be desired to make one wise, she took of the fruit thereof, and did eat, and gave also unto her husband with her; and he did eat. And the eyes of them both were opened, and they knew that they were naked; and they sewed fig leaves together, and made themselves aprons (Gen. 3:4–7).

Both the immediate effect of the fruit on Adam and Eve, and words of the Divine discussion after the Fall had taken place make it clear that Satan was, in a limited sense, making a genuine offer:

> And the LORD God said, Behold, the man is become as one of us, to know good and evil: and now, lest he put forth his hand, and take also of the tree of life, and eat, and live for ever (Gen. 3:22).

The fruit of the tree of the knowledge of good and evil did, indeed, impart the promised knowledge to Adam and Eve. It gave them something that they never had before. Implanted within their souls was a knowledge of good and evil, a knowledge that we refer to as the conscience.

The word 'conscience' comes from two Latin words meaning 'together knowledge'. Thus, it has the sense of a knowledge that is shared. The sense of right and wrong that Adam and Eve gained after the Fall was not an arbitrary moral code. Nor was it simply the outworking of a set of evolutionary impulses. Man, God said, 'is become as one of us'. Adam and Eve had acquired a knowledge that they shared with God – an understanding of right and wrong that imparted to them an understanding of the Divine moral standard.

The Epistle to the Romans helps us to understand the revelation of conscience more clearly. In the opening chapters of the epistle, Paul's argument demonstrates that 'all the world [is] guilty before God' (Rom. 3:19). In order to prove that conclusion, Paul must show that both Jew and Gentile, alike, are sinners, that they have fallen short of God's requirements. Insofar as the Jew is concerned, this presents no difficulty. The Jews had the Divinely-given Law, and their sin was manifest by their failure to obey that Law. But what of the Gentiles of the pagan world, who had received no special revelation from God? How could they be expected to know and to obey God? On what basis could they be judged? Paul identifies two sources of revelation that are available to all.

The first of these sources is the witness of Creation to the character of God:

> Because that which may be known of God is manifest in them; for God hath shewed it unto them. For the invisible things of Him from the Creation of the world are clearly seen, being understood by the things that are made, even His eternal power and Godhead; so that they are without excuse (Rom. 1:19–20).

The splendour of Creation, then, lets us see the power and greatness of God. It is not a comprehensive revelation, but it does allow man to know enough about God to realise that He should be glorified for Who He is, and thanked for what He does (Rom. 1:21).

Additional to this revelation of God in Creation, is the revelation of conscience. Like the creatorial revelation, the revelation tells us something about the character of God. It is not now God's power and greatness that are revealed, but His moral character:

> For not the hearers of the law are just before God, but the doers of the law shall be justified. For when the Gentiles, which have not the law, do by nature the things contained in the law, these, having not the law, are a law unto themselves: which shew the work of the law written in their hearts, their conscience also bearing witness, and their thoughts the mean while accusing or else excusing one another (Rom. 2:13–15).

The circumstances of the Gentiles about whom Paul spoke are congruent with those of antediluvian man. Within their souls was a conscience that allowed them to share God's knowledge of what was right and what was wrong. Not even the most intelligent members of the animal Creation shared this internal guide – man alone was the possessor of this moral compass. Ever since, man has had an inbuilt sense of right and wrong.

Responsibility

In the light of this revelation, man's responsibility was clear. As in the dispensation of innocence, there was no difficulty in decoding a complex set of demands – God's requirements were simple. The revelation of God in Creation brought with it an imperative to acknowledge His existence, to worship Him, and to be thankful for the bounty of His provision. In addition, the double revelation of conscience brought with it a double responsibility. Man knew good and evil and was, accordingly, responsible to do that which was good and not to do that which was evil.

Man's responsibility, in the dispensation of conscience, was simple. Yet he proved utterly incapable of discharging that responsibility. The revelation of conscience serves only to emphasise the sinfulness of fallen humanity. The tragedy and the treachery of Satan's temptation were contained in the fact that the knowledge of good and evil imparted no ability to do the good, or to eschew the evil. Adam, Eve, and their succeeding generations had the light of conscience but, in the absence of accompanying spiritual life, they failed utterly to live in that light and to obey the revelation that had been imparted by God and implanted within their souls.

REBELLION

The failure of humanity to discharge the responsibility that God had laid upon it becomes clear almost from the commencement of the dispensation. In Cain's self-willed rebellion against God we see the very prototype of fallen man in his waywardness and lawlessness. That rebellion was expressed, first of all, in his failure to offer to God an acceptable sacrifice. As we have already noted, Cain did not offer an unacceptable sacrifice through accident, stupidity, or bad luck. Rather, his offering of the fruits of the earth was an act of defiance. Like the generations of men since, Cain wanted to approach God on his own terms, and in a way that emphasised his works, his labour, and his achievement.

Cain's failure to worship God appropriately was followed by a failure to obey the dictates of conscience. It is telling that the first sin recorded in this dispensation is both the first murder, and the first fratricide. Cain's action did not fall into a moral grey area. Even in our relativistic, post modern world, where the existence of moral absolutes is routinely denied, we would expect unanimous consent that what Cain did was wrong. Surely his conscience must have screamed a warning as he raised his hand to slay his brother. And yet Cain did not listen and did not obey, and Abel lay dead as an eloquent testimony to the failure and the sin of man.

Cain's sin, and the events that followed it, also demonstrate an important feature of conscience. 1 Timothy 4:2 speaks of a seared conscience and, while it does so in a different context, we can see evidence of a seared conscience in Cain's behaviour. We can substantiate, from our own experience, the fact that conscience does not always speak with equal volume. When we override our conscience we find that the power of its promptings becomes progressively less. After a very little time we find ourselves committing with total unconcern sins that once filled us with an acute sense of guilt. Once Cain had disobeyed his conscience, he started on a downward road. He would reject the opportunity for repentance that God graciously offered, and ultimately he would go 'out from the presence of the Lord' (Gen. 4:16) a renegade apostate, in flagrant rebellion against his Creator.

Cain's initial sin was shocking in its motivation, and appalling in its violence. Sadly, though, it was only the beginning of what fallen man would do. As we have already seen, six generations would produce a Lamech, who boasted of his vengeful killing, and resolved to excel his notorious ancestor in his arrogant violence. The descent was rapid and irresistible. Only sixteen hundred years passed before God's eyes found only one righteous man amongst a sinful wicked race.

That race was sinful in its outward actions and in its inner being:

> And God saw that the wickedness of man was great in the earth, and that every imagination of the thoughts of his heart was only evil continually (Gen. 6:5).

Moreover, it was deaf not just to the voice of conscience, but to the strivings of the Spirit of God. The scale of their wickedness is difficult for us to imagine, but we get a sense of the utter moral bankruptcy of the antediluvian world in the response of God to His survey of humanity:

> It repented the LORD that He had made man on the earth, and it grieved Him at His heart. And the LORD said, I will destroy man whom I have created from the face of the earth; both man, and beast, and the creeping thing, and the fowls of the air; for it repenteth Me that I have made them (Gen. 6:6–7).

Man was utterly corrupt, and the Creation of which he was head, and which had been pronounced by God to be 'very good' had, with him, become polluted and distorted. So vile a world needed not social reform, but a complete rebooting. Only a radical judgement could bring the needed cleansing.

Retribution

That judgement came in the form of the Flood. Perhaps no Biblical event has so often been so misrepresented as 'Noah's Flood'. Countless children's books have depicted the ark bobbing on clear blue water, as Mr and Mrs Noah and a few attendant animals beam cheerfully. True, the giraffes not uncommonly appear to be somewhat cramped for headroom in their temporary accommodation, but minor concerns like these aside, it seems like a pretty idyllic scene.

Nothing could be further from the truth of the event. For forty days and forty nights the world was engulfed in a raging torrent of water. It came pelting down with tremendous force from above, it came welling up with terrifying violence from below. The face of the globe was dramatically altered and it seems not unlikely that it was at this point that the earth's axis of rotation acquired its

24° tilt. At the same time, billions of human beings, and countless animals were drowned beneath the encroaching water. In the ark, and in spite of the stability built into its design, Noah his family and the animals that they carried must have experienced a rough ride as the world around them was submerged in judgement of unutterable and unimaginable ferocity. There are five aspects of this judgement that demand our consideration – its authenticity, its scale, its scope, its effects, and the grace displayed in it.

The Authenticity of the Judgement

For generations scientists have debated the authenticity and reliability of the Biblical narrative of the Flood. Since the publication, in 1961, of Whitcomb and Morris's *The Genesis Flood: The Biblical Record and its Scientific Implications*, Flood geologists have increasingly drawn attention to the way in which significant aspects of earth's geology can be accounted for by the processes that would have taken place during a cataclysmic deluge of Biblical proportions. Their work, and that of Flood geologists in general, is interesting and suggestive, but it is not our concern here. Rather, it is sufficient for us to note that Peter (1 Pet. 3:20; 2 Pet. 2:3–7), the writer to the Hebrews (ch. 11), and pre-eminently the Lord Jesus Christ Himself (Mt. 24:27–28; Lk. 17:26–27) attest to the authenticity and historicity of the account of the Flood given in Genesis.

The Scale of the Judgement

As we have already seen, the Flood was far more than the result of forty days' heavy rain. Instead, there were two unique aspects that separate this deluge from any merely local Flood, however devastating it might be. Genesis 7:11 tells us that 'all the fountains of the great deep [were] broken up, and the windows of heaven were opened'.

These were one-off events, that were not, and that could not be repeated. The search for the origins of the water that came through the open windows of Heaven takes us back to Genesis 1:

> And God said, Let there be a firmament in the midst of the waters, and let it divide the waters from the waters. And God made the firmament, and divided the waters which were under the firmament from the waters which were above the firmament: and it was so. And God called the firmament Heaven. And the evening and the morning were the second day (v.7).

In other words, God had created the world so that it was surrounded by the atmosphere – the firmament or 'expanse' – just as it is today. Above this was a layer of water – the waters above the firmament. It was these waters that, during the Flood, rushed with deathly force through the windows of Heaven. We do not have a similar Scripture to explain what is meant by the breaking up of the fountains of the great deep, but it seems reasonable to infer that this great deep was a vast sub-terranean store of water that was forcibly released during the trauma of the Flood.

It is striking that God had made provision in the Creation for the judgement of the world. This emphasises the point that we have already noted repeatedly. God is never overtaken by circumstances, and He is never reduced to reacting in panic or desperation to events. Far in advance of Noah, in an Eternity before Adam and Eve ever existed, His purposes stood fast.

The Scope of the Judgement

The New Testament references to the Flood that we have noted makes it clear that the account given in

Genesis 7 is not a garbled retelling of a pre-existing legend of a local Flood. The Flood covered the whole world, it destroyed all of the world that then was. It was global in its scope, and universal in its effects. The scale of sin's contagion was measured by the scope of God's judgement. God had vowed 'I will destroy man whom I have created from the face of the earth; both man, and beast, and the creeping thing, and the fowls of the air' (Gen. 6:7). Speaking to Noah He revealed the radical nature of the impending judgement:

> The end of all flesh is come before Me; for the earth is filled with violence through them; and, behold, I will destroy them with the earth (Gen. 6:13).

Genesis 7:19–23 provides us with a clear and uncompromising account of the Flood's scope that makes it impossible for us to argue that this was any sort of limited judgement:

> And the waters prevailed exceedingly upon the earth; and all the high hills, that were under the whole heaven, were covered. Fifteen cubits upward did the waters prevail; and the mountains were covered. And all flesh died that moved upon the earth, both of fowl, and of cattle, and of beast, and of every creeping thing that creepeth upon the earth, and every man: All in whose nostrils was the breath of life, of all that was in the dry land, died. And every living substance was destroyed which was upon the face of the ground, both man, and cattle, and the creeping things, and the fowl of the heaven; and they were destroyed from the earth: and Noah only remained alive, and they that were with him in the ark.

The Effects of the Judgement

The effects of the Flood, then, were global. In physical terms, the erosive action of the rapidly moving water and the effects of the tremendous pressure involved in the Flood have left an indelible mark upon the crust of the globe, upon its continents and its rocks. The removal of the waters above the firmament would have dramatically changed the environment on earth, and some of these changes are reflected in the changes in human lifestyle after the Flood.

In human and in spiritual terms, the Flood brought to an end the line of Cain. That line had continued in the Godless direction set by its progenitor, and existed in permanent and implacable rebellion against God. Now it was brought to an end. There is no one alive today who has a genetic link with the Cainic line. Sadly, although Cain has no physical descendants, he has many spiritual heirs, even unto this present day.

Along with the line of Cain, the results of broken down separation were brought to an end. Whatever the precise nature and history of the mighty giants, in their hybrid monstrosity, they, too, came to an end at the Flood.

Thus it is that, when the crew of the ark stepped forth onto dry land, they stepped into a new world. It had been cleansed of all that defiled, and they, too, had been separated from all that went before. It was a good start, but we know too well the sad and sordid story of a new world spoiled, and the repetition of the sorry cycle of human sin and failure.

The Grace Displayed in Judgement

At the close of the dispensation of innocence the judgement of God was tempered by His grace and mercy. So it is, too, with this second dispensation. Righteous judgement fell, but God moved in grace, preserving Noah and his family, and through them the human race. For, while it is true that 'Noah was a just man and perfect in his generations, and Noah walked with God' (Gen. 6:9), so too it is the case that 'Noah found grace in the eyes of the Lord' (v.8). Noah's righteousness could not have saved him – his salvation was 'by grace, through faith' (Eph. 2:8). And, just as the judgement that brought the first dispensation to a close contained hints at deliverance to come, so too, God does not allow the culminating judgement of this dispensation to fall before He has given a commitment regarding the future to Noah. It was before the Flood came, before the ark was built that God promised:

> But with thee will I establish my covenant; and thou shalt come into the ark, thou, and thy sons, and thy wife, and thy sons' wives with thee (Gen. 6:18).

Noah was about to enter a time of unimaginable trauma. He and his family would be tossed like corks on the face of the ocean. Almost a year of total disorientation, uncertainty, and fear was about to begin. But God would not send him into that experience unarmed by a promise. At the darkest and most difficult hours of his experience, Noah was able to hold on to the promise of God, and to look forward to its inevitable and assured fulfilment.

Noah's experience is not the only manifestation of Divine grace during this dispensation. Centuries before the onslaught of the first waters of the Flood, God had miraculously removed a man from a world that was under judgement.

> By faith Enoch was translated that he should not see death; and was not found, because God had translated him: for before his translation he had this testimony, that he pleased God (Heb. 11:5).

Enoch knew something of coming judgement. To his son he gave the name Methuselah, meaning 'when he is gone, it shall come to pass'. And, in the year that Methuselah died, it did come to pass. But Enoch never experienced the judgement that he had anticipated. Noah and his family would be saved through the judgement, Enoch was saved away from the judgement.

What a lovely anticipation this is of the dispensation of grace. We who are saved, who walk with God, know that there is judgement to fall on this world. We do not fear it, for 'God hath not appointed us to wrath, but to obtain salvation by our Lord Jesus Christ' (1 Thess. 5:9). He is our Deliverer from the wrath to come (1 Thess. 1:10), and before ever its waves begin to break, we shall have been translated – raptured in a moment to be with our risen Lord. Noah's experience was a different one. He was preserved in the ark, but he knew, as Enoch never did, the buffeting of the waves, the roaring of the waters. He was preserved through the judgement just as, in a coming day, a faithful Jewish remnant will be preserved through the terrors of the Tribulation judgement that will bring this dispensation to its close. Thus, the Flood judgement of the world was preceded by a double display of the grace of God in rescuing those who walked with Him.

CHAPTER 9

THE DISPENSATION OF HUMAN GOVERNMENT

OF ALL THE tasks and duties that mark the cycle of the agricultural year, there are few so invigorating as the release of young calves into pasture for the first time. Having spent their short lives in the confined quarters of shed and pen, it takes the animals a little time to comprehend the reality of their new world. Stunned by the space, they step gingerly forward, expecting to reach a barrier. One faltering step follows another until gradually the truth of their freedom dawns, bringing an ecstasy of exhilaration. Leaping and kicking, they stream across the verdant sward, in a heart-lifting celebration of life and vigour.

It is not, perhaps, taking too great a licence to imagine that a similar scene, on a far larger scale, must have taken place on Mount Ararat, when the great door of the ark finally opened. An encyclopaedic collection of animals had spent months cooped up in what can hardly have been other than cramped, dark, and noisome conditions. Now they were leaving these behind to issue forth into a new world, under new skies. Their old habitats had been utterly eradicated, but in the varied climates and environments of this judged world, God had provided a niche where each species could flourish and prosper. Set free from the ark, they must have streamed down the face of Ararat like a tidal wave of life, carrying the Creator's handiwork to the remotest recesses of His world.

For Noah, the experience must have been rather different. No doubt he too was glad to exchange the fetid air of the ark for the breezes of the mountain top. He must surely have looked with wild surmise on this new world, so different in its rugged majesty from what he had known. But for Noah, this new world shouted the terror of Divine judgement. Every crevasse, every gorge was eloquent of the mighty power of the deluge, the enveloping sky, looking so different now that the waters above the firmament had vanished, was an unavoidable reminder of the awful ferocity with which cascading torrents had sluiced through the open windows of heaven. Noah could scarcely be blamed if he left the safety of the ark with a heart in which misgivings and fear held sway.

But these emotions can hardly have been unmixed with hope. Before the Flood, God had promised Noah that He would establish His covenant with him, and that promise, which must have powerfully sustained Noah through the darkness of the deluge, was about to be fulfilled. Noah stepped from the ark to an interview with God, and was about to be introduced to an unknown – and astounding – aspect of God's character.

Revelation

The revelations of previous dispensations had already manifested much of God's character. His goodness and grace, as well as His righteousness had been demonstrated beyond doubt. Now, however, Noah was about to learn a new aspect of God's character. God was revealing Himself, for the first time, as a covenant-making God.* That fact is not a minor detail or an obscure quibble. It is an amazing and astounding truth that should cause us to wonder and to worship at the vastness of God's grace.

God had already promised to establish His covenant with Noah. Now, on the cleansed soil of a judged earth, the Creator enters, for the first time, into covenant relationship with His creature. To appreciate the significance of this, we need to understand what a covenant is. A covenant is more than a promise. It is a legal agreement that gives a solemn and binding force to commitments made by the parties involved. The example of a covenant with which we are most familiar is marriage. Being married is more than the exchange of promises between a man and a woman. It involves a legally binding agreement, and a recognised and socially agreed format. In the world of the Old Testament, before mass literacy or the existence of a stable legal system, covenants were an essential part of life at all levels, from kings downwards. Now God uses the concepts and vocabulary of earth to emphasise the force and the certainty of the commitments that He was making to humanity.

It is worth noting that the Hebrew word translated 'covenant' has, according to some scholars, the root idea

---

* A number of commentators, perhaps most influentially C.I. Scofield, have suggested that the revelation from God to Adam in Eden and after the Fall constitute respectively the Edenic and Adamic covenants. However, a number of considerations weigh against this view. Firstly, Scripture does not describe these revelations as covenants. (Although it should be noted that quite a number of translations render Hosea 6:7 as 'But they like Adam have transgressed the covenant' ['But they like men have transgressed the covenant' KJV]. However, the translation presents considerable difficulties, and their evidence is hardly conclusive.) Secondly, the explicit covenants follow a definite structure – which they share with legal covenants between men. Thirdly, these revelations have less to do with God making commitments to man, and more to do with the responsibilities of mankind.

of a fetter or a bond.* This etymology recognizes that a covenant was an agreement that bound two parties together. This emphasises the fact that the making of a covenant implies a commitment. Making a commitment is costly. When we enter into covenant commitment with someone, we are, to a greater or lesser degree, in bondage to that person. We sacrifice our freedom, some of our independence. This fact lies, for example, at the root of the modern attitude to marriage. Many men and women wish to enjoy the privileges of marriage, without its costs, and so they baulk at commitment, refusing to sacrifice their independence by entering into the covenant of marriage.

Against this backdrop, the wonder of the covenants of God appears more clearly. In grace and condescension that we can hardly estimate the Almighty God of eternity has committed Himself – formally and irrevocably – to mankind. It serves further to underline God's grace that His covenants are often unilateral. Men's covenants bilaterally bind kingdom to kingdom, tribe to tribe, or man to wife. By contrast, God's covenants are largely one-sided – in grace He deigns to bind Himself to mankind. As history unfolded, God moved repeatedly to establish His covenants with mankind. This Noahic covenant, then, is just the first of God's great acts of commitment to humanity.

It is precious to note that the terms of God's covenant were designed to address and allay Noah's most immediate concerns and his most pressing fears. He had just passed through an immensely traumatic experience. The solid ground upon which he had stood throughout his life had, quite literally, been swept away by a mighty

---

* See the discussion in René Lopez, 'Israelite Covenants in the Light of Ancient Near Eastern Covenants (Part 1 of 2)', *CTS Journal*, 9 (2003), 92–111

torrent. The stability and reliability of earth, with her seasons and her years had been shaken to the very core. Having experienced this, Noah must have wondered if normal life would ever be possible again. Would he and his descendants go about in constant dread of another cataclysm, always on tenterhooks lest God upend Creation once more? It is hardly surprising, then, that Noah's first action was to offer a sacrifice, to seek to propitiate the God Whose power had been so clearly seen. So it is, that for the first time in the record of Scripture, we read of a sweet savour ascending from an earthly altar to thenostrils of God. And, as the fragrance that foretold the offering of Christ reached the presence of God, we are allowed to see something of the Divine purpose for the planet:

> And the LORD smelled a sweet savour; and the LORD said in His heart, I will not again curse the ground any more for man's sake; for the imagination of man's heart is evil from his youth; neither will I again smite any more every thing living, as I have done. While the earth remaineth, seedtime and harvest, and cold and heat, and summer and winter, and day and night shall not cease (Gen. 8:21–22).

God did not enter into covenant with mankind on the basis of a naïve belief that the experience of the Flood had fundamentally improved his character. God knew that after, as before, the Flood, the imagination of man's heart was irretrievably evil. There would never be any shortage of reason to pour out a further deluge of Divine punishment upon the earth. But, with this knowledge, God binds Himself by a great commitment to the race, and to the planet. The global cataclysm of the Flood would not be repeated; day and night, seedtime and harvest would continue without interruption while the earth remained. It was this purpose that was codified and expressed in the covenant made with Noah. The making of that covenant commenced with God's blessing upon Noah and his sons, and its details spoke of His careful provision for His Creation.

The first element of God's revelation to Noah dealt with humanity's relationship with Creation. Mankind still occupied a unique position in relation to the animal Creation, but his dominion was far less benign than the conditions that had obtained in Eden. Now man's mastery over the animals was ensured and enforced by their fear of him. That mastery extended, for the first time, to the eating of the animals for food. Perhaps because of the changed demands that a new ecology made upon man's body, the vegetarianism of the antediluvian world was replaced with an omnivorous provision of flesh and herbs. But the freedom to eat meat was not absolute. Man was not to eat 'the flesh with the life thereof, which is the blood thereof' (9:4). The taking of animal life was not to be vicious, wanton, or animalistic. It was to be done to meet the needs of man, and to be done carefully and humanely.

The revelation also addressed man's relationship with man. Again, it is clear that the Fall had not eradicated humanity's uniqueness in God's creatorial order. Man was fallen, but not to the level of the beasts. Human life has a value different to and greater than animal life. The purpose of Divinely mandated human government was to safeguard that value. The introduction of capital punishment here stands in contrast to the revenge killings that had been a feature under the previous dispensation. Now God delegated authority to man to execute that punishment. It is important to note that capital punishment was not instituted by God primarily as a deterrent. Nor did it represent a devaluing of human life. Rather, the reverse is true. The gravity of the penalty demonstrates the enormity of the crime and accordingly emphasises the unique value of human life. And God mandated the increase of that human life – the human race was to be 'fruitful and multiply; bring forth abundantly in the earth and multiply therein' (Gen. 9:7).

The Divine standards and values embodied in the Noahic covenant are vitally important in the age in which we live. Twenty-first century society seems to be sadly confused about the value of life. We cannot be indifferent to the pleas of animal rights campaigners that animals be treated humanely. However, we cannot for a moment accede to their contention that animal life is of equal value to human life. Nor can we are we able to adopt the estimation of the value of human life that can calmly contemplate the mass murder of thousands of unborn infants in the name of social convenience. Our society has a great deal to say about human dignity and respect, and pillories Scripture and those who hold its truth as barbaric and unsophisticated. But when the values of the Noahic covenant are placed alongside the notions of our own seriously sick society it is not difficult to see which the contrast favours.

Finally, God's revelation addressed man's relationship to God, and here we have the making of the covenant. This covenant was unconditional. God had laid requirements upon man in the earlier verses of the chapter, but He does not make His covenant conditional upon man's response to these requirements. It was an everlasting (v.16) and an extensive covenant. God made a clear commitment to Noah, his seed, and 'to every beast of the earth' (v.10). The purpose of God, revealed at the close of chapter 8, is now embodied in the promise of God, and the fears and concerns of Noah and his family are addressed by the grace of God:

> And I will establish My covenant with you; neither shall all flesh be cut off any more by the waters of a

Flood; neither shall there any more be a Flood to destroy the earth (Gen. 9:11).

God's promise was clear and unambiguous – reverently speaking, God was not leaving His options open, was not providing Himself with an escape clause. His commitment was absolute. And that commitment was confirmed by a most wonderful sign:

> And God said, This is the token of the covenant which I make between Me and you and every living creature that is with you, for perpetual generations: I do set My bow in the cloud, and it shall be for a token of a covenant between Me and the earth. And it shall come to pass, when I bring a cloud over the earth, that the bow shall be seen in the cloud: And I will remember My covenant, which is between Me and you and every living creature of all flesh; and the waters shall no more become a Flood to destroy all flesh. And the bow shall be in the cloud; and I will look upon it, that I may remember the everlasting covenant between God and every living creature of all flesh that is upon the earth (Gen. 9:12–16).

This sign is a glorious expression of the greatness and grace of our God. With consummate artistry and ineffable skill, He engineered the atmospheric conditions of the post-diluvian world so that the darkest clouds and the heaviest torrents would be accompanied by a beautiful bow that spoke, and speaks, and will ever speak of hope, of security, and of the unalterable covenant of God. Noah and his family had never experienced rain before the Flood. The first shower after they left the ark must have filled them with trepidation. But as they looked up, and saw the rays of the hidden sun scattered into a brilliant band of colour, they were reassured. They were remembering God's everlasting covenant with Noah. And, notwithstanding the doom and despair so confidently proclaimed by the climatologists of our own day we, too, can remember and rejoice in God's everlasting covenant that still stands steadfast, unbroken – and unbreakable.

Responsibility

As we have seen, the Noahic covenant was unilateral and unconditional. However, God's revelation to Noah did place responsibilities upon mankind. Essentially, these responsibilities fell into two categories. Mankind was to multiply, and fill the earth (9:1, 7), and man was to establish social order and justice, to ensure the punishment of murderers. These were hardly onerous requirements, and they spoke of God's purpose for mankind, as well as His care for the race. They underlined the unique dignity that pertained to humanity. They were, furthermore, designed for the benefit of man, for the stability and order of society. And yet, the dispensation had hardly got under way before man's failure had begun to manifest itself. Too soon, we see the man into whose hands government had been committed lying naked in a drunken stupor in his tent. And that was just the beginning of an inexorable slide not just towards a failure to discharge Divinely mandated responsibilities, but to an outright rebellion against the ordinances of God.

Rebellion

As with the Flood, the judgement that brought to an end the dispensation of human government is often misrepresented and misunderstood. And we fail to understand the judgement because we fail to understand the nature and the scale of the rebellion that prompted it. The resolve of the world's population to build 'a city and a tower, whose top may reach unto heaven' (Gen. 11:4) sounds like the laughable dream of an unsophisticated and backward civilisation, and hardly seems to merit the Divine judgement that was meted out upon it. To look at the tower of Babel in this way is to fail to grasp both its context and its significance.

It is important to understand the relationship between Genesis chapters 10 and 11. In Genesis 10:5, the emergence of nations is simply stated:

> By these were the isles of the Gentiles divided in their lands; every one after his tongue, after their families, in their nations.

As is demonstrated by the mention of tongues here, chapter 11 does not follow chapter 10 chronologically. Rather, it is a parenthesis that expands upon and explains the terse statement of chapter 10. With this in mind, the references to Babel in chapter 10 assume a particular importance in helping us to understand precisely what it was that was judged at Babel.

We discover that there was a particular association between Nimrod and Babel. Nimrod is described as both 'a mighty one' and a 'mighty hunter' (Gen. 10:8, 9) and Babel was 'the beginning of his kingdom' (v.10). This, then, was a man of heroic proportions, a man of massive ability. His character and his abilities were such as to distinguish him from the rest of humanity. Here, in the remote mists of time, emerged the first charismatic world leader. The governmental responsibility that was given to humanity seems, now, to have been vested in this remarkable man. But what was the character of his rule?

That question is, of course, clearly answered by the events of chapter 11. But even before Nimrod's reign blossoms into full-blown rebellion against God, sufficient details are provided to make it clear that this man, though great, stood in opposition to God and all that was of God.

As is the case with many of the characters in the Old Testament, Nimrod's name gives us a significant clue to his character. There has been much scholarly debate and disagreement about the origins of Nimrod's name, but there is also a consensus amongst Old Testament scholars that, whatever its origins, in Hebrew Nimrod means 'a rebel'. He was well named. As we shall see, both his personal conduct and the kingdom that he established and ruled were in rebellion against God. Nimrod disobeyed the Divine commands given in the covenant with Noah. He set himself in opposition to God, with a steely determination to rewrite history, to enthrone man, and to thwart God. Then as now, rebellion was a sin peculiarly obnoxious to God, and Nimrod personified rebellion.

Nor is Nimrod's name the only indication of his character. Genesis 10:9 describes Nimrod as a 'mighty hunter before the Lord'. The meaning of this phrase has been the subject of much debate and no little speculation. What it means to be a mighty hunter 'before the Lord' is not clear. The expression could mean something like 'in the view of the Lord', which is essentially the reading adopted by the translators of the King James Version, and by most other translations of Scripture. This reading also provides a sensible translation of the earlier use of the expression in Genesis 6:11 ('The earth also was corrupt before God'). However, some commentators favour the translation 'in the face of the Lord', or 'against the Lord'. This reading also makes a reasonable amount of sense in the context of Genesis 6, and seems to fit with the general view of Nimrod's character.

However we might choose to interpret 'before the Lord', we should not allow it to distract our attention from the fact that Nimrod was 'a mighty hunter'. As we have seen, the Noahic covenant inaugurated a significant change in humanity's relationship with Creation. Now, for the first time, man had permission to take animal life in order to provide food. But we have also noted that this permission was hedged with caveats that forbade man to slay animals wantonly or cruelly. Yet Nimrod is renowned for his ability in the hunting of game. For his own enjoyment, and to establish his fame, he transgressed the terms of the Divine covenant, and demonstrated his rebellion against God. The otherwise obscure words of Genesis 10:9 acquire a clearer meaning when we understand this. Scripture is making it clear that it was upon this defiance of God's Word that Nimrod's fame was based. It was his defining characteristic. And, in the admiring words of this oft-repeated and proverbial epithet, we see, too, the sorts of act and the type of values that were deemed admirable in the decaying world of the dispensation of human government.

Nimrod's assumption of despotic leadership – however achieved – is also eloquent of his rebellion. Again, human government was instituted by God in the Noahic covenant. It was designed to impose order and justice upon society, to prevent the indiscriminate perpetuation of violence by violence. But in this regard, too, Nimrod distorts and exceeds the terms of God's covenant. Under Nimrod, human government ceased to be the means of maintaining the order of society and maintaining the sanctity of human life, and became a means to the exultation of man and the dethroning of God.

This was the character of the man who reigned at Babel, and the record of Genesis 11 makes it clear that this character, the character of inveterate rebellion, was firmly stamped upon the men of Babel and their ambitious but blasphemous project.

The account given in Genesis 11 makes the scale of this rebellion clear. Five times over in the story the phrase 'all the earth' appears (11:1, 4, 8, 9 [x2]). United under the effective leadership of Nimrod, mankind set about rearing the ultimate monument to himself, embodying in brick and slime not just his corrupt religion, but his vainglorious pride (v.4).

That project was not a naïve design to build a tower that reached to Heaven. It was to build a city and a tower. Most scholars agree that this tower was most likely a ziggurat – one of the stepped pyramids the remains of which have been uncovered in the Mesopotamian valley. 'These stepped structures were built in Babylonian cities to replicate the concept of a sacred mountain where humanity and divinity could commune.'* Something of the nature of this tower can be seen in the seven-stage ziggurat with a temple to the god Marduk at the top called *e-temen-an-ki*, or 'the temple of the platform between heaven and earth', which was built in the city of Babylon sometime during the 6th or 7th century BC. Like *e-temen-an-ki*, this proto-Babylonian tower was no mere architectural folly or the delusional engineering project of a simple and unsophisticated people. Rather, it was the idolatrous temple of the false Babylonian religion. Babel was designed to be both the civic and religious head-quarters of the Babylonian empire, and to ensure the unity of her people, and their lasting fame.

Beyond this, the tower was designed to ensure that those who built it would not be scattered abroad upon the face of the whole earth. In their journeying from the east, the human race had arrived at the plain of Shinar.

---

* James McKeown, *Genesis*, (Grand Rapids, MI: William B. Eerdmans ,2008), 71

Here, in the heart of the Fertile Crescent, they found the inviting environs that they sought. Here they would remain, and their monumental construction would be a focal point and a rallying centre that would ensure that they would never be 'scattered abroad over the face of the whole earth' (v.4). Their plan seemed a sensible one. However, it was in direct contradiction of what God had ordained in His covenant with Noah. Once in relation to the animals (8:19), and twice in relation to mankind (9:1, 7) God had given the command to be fruitful, and multiply, and replenish the earth. His intention was for mankind to repopulate the whole of the globe, to spread throughout its climes and zones, to find a home in every part. But, in their arrogance, mankind felt that they knew better. They had found a comfortable and commodious dwelling place, and God's command was to be no impediment to their settling down there. Their reasoning, informed as it was by natural considerations, was specious. Their plan seemed to make perfect sense. But it was just another indication of their disregard for God and of their rebellion against their Creator.

The audacity of mankind's rebellion at Babel was great, and the severity of God's judgement confirms this abundantly for us. But their rebellion has a significance beyond the events that took place way back in the remoter mists of time. And that significance becomes clear as we think of the elements of their rebellion. We have traced the emergence of a charismatic and powerful world leader. We have seen how his considerable abilities were all channelled in rebellion against God. We have also noted how his rebellion infected all of humanity, and how mankind gathered together to rear a city and an idolatrous temple. And linked with all is one of the most resonant, one of the most notorious names in all of Scripture – Babylon. What we see at Babel was not brought to an end by Divine judgement. Rather, it has lived on through history as the dark and sin-stained narrative of man's rebellion against God, and of man's corruption, distortion, and counterfeit of what is of God. In Nimrod, we have the first antichrist, a chilling picture of the Antichrist, and in Babel we have a prototype of the Babylonian programme that will one day culminate in a temple and a city which will be the unifying centre for the whole earth. The rebellion that marked the dispensation of human government is historical – it actually happened, just as Scripture says. It is also typical, and it foreshadows what will happen in a greater and climactic rebellion that is yet to come.

Retribution

No one who knows anything of God would entertain, even for a moment, the idea that His judgement upon mankind at Babel was wanton or disproportionate. Even if we were tempted to do so, however, the Scriptural account is designed to stress that this was condign punishment – just and appropriate to the crime.

The narrative of Genesis 11:1-9 has been carefully constructed to emphasise the way in which Divine punishment addresses human action. So, for example, the men of Babel twice preface their plans with the phrase 'Go to' (v.3, 4). Similarly, in verse 7, God's statement of His intention to judge is introduced in the same way. The human intention was thwarted, their confident plans never reached fruition. But when God says 'go to', the course of action that He outlines is irresistible in its force, and inevitable in its success. Similarly, in verse 5, the Babelites had expressed their intention to avoid being 'scattered abroad over the face of the whole earth'. By contrast, verses 8 and 9 both repeat the same phrase as a summary of the results of God's judgement. The very thing that the men of Babel, in disobedience to God's command, had resolved to prevent was the inescapable outcome of judgement. Finally, the narrative clearly identifies the common language of mankind as the source of their social and physical unity. This feature of the world of Babel is mentioned right at the commencement of the narrative, in 11:1. In verse 6, the LORD highlights the importance of their shared language and in verse 7 declares His purpose to confuse it. Like every other purpose of God, this is accomplished, as verse 9 makes clear.

The account given in these verses divides into three sections. We have the words of the men of Babel (vv. 1–4) followed by the words of God (vv. 5–7) and the actions of God (vv. 8–9). This structure emphasises for us the vast gap between the power of man and the power of God. The men of Babel were very clear, very confident in their plans, and yet, apart from a mention of their building in verse 5, we hear nothing about the accomplishment of those plans. By contrast, the plans articulated by God match up exactly with His actions and their outcomes. The might of God and the futility of man are dramatically and tellingly juxtaposed, and we seem to hear the echo of God's laughter as He derides the people who 'imagine a vain thing' (Ps. 2:1–2).

Indeed, the story is not without a flavour of ironic humour. Verse 5, quite strikingly, tells us that God 'came down to see the city and the tower'. Clearly, this is anthropomorphism – human characteristics are being attributed to God. The implication of the words is clear enough. This great engineering feat that has been the boast of the world and that was to reach up to heaven is, in reality, so insignificant as to require God to come down from Heaven if He is to see it. This statement, along with the words of verse 7 ('Go to, let us go down') is also a reminder that, in spite of the Babelites' intention to uprear a temple for their gods, 'God that made the world and all things therein, seeing that he is Lord of heaven and earth, dwelleth not in temples made with hands; neither is worshipped with men's hands, as though he needed any thing, seeing he giveth to all life, and breath, and all things' (Acts 17:24–25).

The judgement of God, then, was both righteous and proportional. It was also exceedingly effective. Without a common language, humanity no longer maintained its common purpose. As those who spoke the same language began to cluster together, nations formed. Particular genetic traits became marked in each group, leading to the expression of ethnic identity.[*] The shared environment and experiences of each group led to the development and expression of a distinctive culture. Even today, as the various movements of cultural nationalism and the amount of money and effort in attempts to resurrect dead or dying languages demonstrate, language is a crucial factor in forming perpetuating national identity.

The confusion of languages, and the separation of humanity into nations has been an enduring as well as effective judgement. The most comprehensive source of information on known living languages currently includes information on 6,909 different languages.[†] All across the globe, humanity is divided not just into nations, but into tribes and factions. Every age, each century has been marked by deep and intractable nationalistic and ethnic conflict.

---

[*] Given some of the uses that have been made of these early chapters in Genesis, it is worth underlining the fact that the roots of nations, and the differentiation of the peoples of earth can be found at Babel. It is also worth reiterating the point that has often been made: Scripture nowhere speaks of races – Paul made it clear that God 'made of one blood all nations of men for to dwell on all the face of the earth' (Acts 17:26).

[†] http://www.ethnologue.org/

And this situation continues in spite of the constant efforts on the part of mankind to reverse the consequences of Babel. By means of conquest, commerce, and co-operation man has tried again and again to return to the unity that marked the world before the judgement at Babel. At various times, these efforts have been attended by varying degrees of success, but before the history of this world comes to a close, the malignant and rebellious unity of Babel will be replicated. Under the rule of one man, and in the service of a global travesty of religion all the nations will be fused together in impious rebellion.

Like every other age, the dispensation of human government has a sad trajectory. It opens with a man in communication with God, and draws to a close with God disrupting man's communication with man. It begins with man leaving a structure designed by God for the salvation of the race, and closes with God destroying a structure designed by men for their own glorification. But though the dispensation ends in disappointment it does not end in despair. God's purpose cannot be thwarted by human actions. In spite of humanity's rebellion, in spite of man's determination to remain clustered in comfort on the plain of Shinar, God intervenes to ensure that earth's remotest nooks are filled with the race that He created, which He loves, and for which He has purposes of grandeur and glory.

CHAPTER 10

THE DISPENSATION OF PROMISE

GENESIS 12 MARKS a dramatic shift in the Divine account of human history. Chapters 1–11 tell the history of the whole human race, and embrace over 2,000 years of history. Now, the writer zooms in, focusing on individuals and on the events that made up their lives. The remaining chapters of the book provide us with a series of biographies – of Abraham, Isaac, Jacob, and Joseph.

The change that takes place at the beginning of Genesis 12 is more than just a change in narrative style. The calling of Abram inaugurates a new dispensation, and marks a fundamental change in the way in which God deals with mankind.*

The scale and significance of this change is marked by the initiative that God takes in calling Abram. In Genesis 1, God had moved, without compulsion or cause to call Creation into being. In the intervening chapters, we see God moving in reaction to the sin and failure of mankind, pronouncing judgement and providing instruction. Now, He moves again, without constraint,

---

* Throughout this chapter, we will use the name Abram when referring to events that took place before Genesis 17, and Abraham for those that took place after.

but in sovereign power to establish a new phase in human history.

That action introduces to us the new and vital concept of election. God selects Abram, and ultimately the nation that descends from him, to fulfil a unique role in His service. Enormous dignity and immense blessing are to be conferred on Abram and his descendants. No reason can be found or given to account for or explain that choice. God is moving in His sovereign and inscrutable authority, selecting the human vessels that will be used to bring His purposes to fruition.

Scripture identifies for us the principle that dominates God's dealings with mankind during this dispensation. The Apostle Paul, writing to the Galatians, describes the 450 years of this dispensation as 'promise' (Gal. 3:16–18). The reason for this is not difficult to see. The dispensation opens with the promises of God and those promises are reiterated to successive generations.

REVELATION

Genesis 12 opens with God speaking to Abram. We have encountered Abram at the end of Genesis 11, but there is nothing to suggest that there is anything remarkable about him, or that he is about to play any significant role in God's purpose. Yet, for all his lack of distinguishing features, Abram is about to hear the voice of God, to receive a Divine command and to be the recipient of Divine blessing. But even before God spoke, Abram had received a remarkable revelation. As Stephen commenced his account of Israel's history, he began not with the words of God, but with His appearing:

> And he said, Men, brethren, and fathers, hearken; The God of glory appeared unto our father

Abraham, when he was in Mesopotamia, before he dwelt in Charran (Acts 7:2).

Abram lived in Mesopotamia, at the very centre of the man's idolatrous religion. He was not weaned from the false gods of His upbringing to the worship and service of the one true God simply by a command. Rather, it was the appearance of God in His glory that had the transforming effect upon Abram. Like the Thessalonian believers, he 'turned to God from idols to serve the living and true God' (1 Thess. 1:9). This is ever the order. It is the magnet of God's glory that empowers the mandate of God's Word. Seldom has this truth been so movingly, and so powerfully stated as in the words of Ora Rowan's beautiful hymn:

> *Hast thou heard Him, seen Him, known Him?*
> *Is not thine a captured heart?*
> *Chief among ten thousand own Him;*
> *Joyful choose the better part.*
>
> *Idols once they won thee, charmed thee,*
> *Lovely things of time and sense;*
> *Gilded thus does sin disarm thee,*
> *Honeyed lest thou turn thee thence.*
>
> *What has stripped the seeming beauty*
> *From the idols of the earth?*
> *Not a sense of right or duty,*
> *But the sight of peerless worth.*
>
> *Not the crushing of those idols,*
> *With its bitter void and smart;*
> *But the beaming of His beauty,*
> *The unveiling of His heart.*

> 'Tis that look that melted Peter,
> 'Tis that face that Stephen saw,
> 'Tis that heart that wept with Mary,
> Can alone from idols draw.

In addition to seeing the glory of God, Abram heard the command of God. That command was strikingly specific in some of its details, and strikingly unspecific in relation to others. The principles of modern marketing would suggest that the most effective way to persuade Abram to leave his home behind would be to stress the benefits of such a move, and to fudge as much as possible the costs involved. The features of his destination would be blazoned in the headline, while the price would occupy a position of decent obscurity well down the page. But God is not a salesman, and He operates in precisely the opposite way. His call is very clear about the cost that His command involves. He lists clearly and uncompromisingly what it is that Abram must leave:

> Now the Lord had said unto Abram, Get thee out of thy country, and from thy kindred, and from thy father's house, unto a land that I will shew thee (Gen. 12:1).

All that was dear and familiar to him, all that contributed to his security, happiness, and sense of identity, must be left behind to answer the call of the God of glory. And, as Abram left, he had no brochure outlining the most attractive features of the land to which he went. He did not even know its name or its location until he had arrived there (v.7). 'He went forth, not knowing whither he went' (Heb. 11:8). As he moved in obedience to God, he moved by faith and not by sight, trusting that the unknown and unseen land promised by God would be worth the sacrifice that he had made.

Abram left home without knowing his destination, but he did not leave without a knowledge of the destiny that God had in store for him. The keynote of that destiny, the dominant theme of the promise of God, was blessing. Five times over in verses 2 and 3, God speaks of the blessing of Abram:

> And I will make of thee a great nation, and I will bless thee, and make thy name great; and thou shalt be a blessing: And I will bless them that bless thee, and curse him that curseth thee: and in thee shall all families of the earth be blessed.

Essentially, these blessings fall into three categories. Abram was promised a land, a seed, and Divine blessing. These blessings would amply compensate Abram for all that he would leave. He was called to leave his country, but God would make of him a great nation. He was called to leave his kindred, the family that formed so vital a part of his identity, but God would make his name great. He was called to leave his father's house, but God would make him a blessing, not to his own family alone, but to all the families of the earth. God is no man's debtor, and while He neither concealed nor minimised the price that Abram had to pay, He made it clear that his reimbursement would be complete and enduring.

It is also noteworthy that the blessings that God, in His sovereign grace, freely bestowed upon Abram answer closely to the aims of man's rebellion at Babel. In Genesis 11:4, the men of Babel stated the central aim of their rebellion: 'let us make us a name'. Their intention was to resist the will of God, to ensure that they would not be 'scattered abroad upon the face of the whole earth'. They sought a great name and a lasting and international legacy. But those blessings were not to be wrested from God by man. At Babel, men sought blessing apart from God. They had relied upon their ingenuity and engineering to provide all that they desired. We have seen the chaos to which their plans were ultimately brought. By contrast, God moves freely to bless Abram, not because he had earned blessing or deserved it, but simply because of the astounding wonder of the grace of God. The contrast between Abram and the men of Babel is further emphasised by Abram's action after he arrived in the land: 'he pitched his tent, having Bethel on the west, and Hai on the east: and there he built an altar unto the Lord, and called upon the name of the Lord' (v.8). As a pilgrim and a stranger, he had no interest in ambitious schemes to uprear permanent and ostentatious structures. What he built for God would endure, his own residence was sufficient but temporary, as befits a man who moved at the command of God.

The blessing of Abram also contrasts with the history recorded in the earlier chapters of Genesis. While those chapters do record the grace of God, their keynote is cursing, and not blessing. Five times over, in those opening chapters we read of Divine cursing. Now, as God moves to inaugurate a distinctively new stage in His dealing with humanity, we have the pronouncement of a five-fold blessing.

As Abram moved from Haran, he took with him the promise of the God Who cannot lie. He could have had no greater basis for his faith. However, as the writer to the Hebrews reminds us, God moved beyond His immutable promise, to make Abram's security doubly secure:

> For when God made promise to Abraham, because he could swear by no greater, he sware by himself, saying , Surely blessing I will bless thee, and multiplying I will multiply thee. And so, after he had patiently endured, he obtained the promise. For men verily swear by the greater: and an oath for

confirmation is to them an end of all strife. Wherein God, willing more abundantly to shew unto the heirs of promise the immutability of His counsel, confirmed it by an oath (Heb. 6:13–17).

In Genesis 12, Abram received the promise of God. Nothing could have been more sure than this, for God cannot lie, and will inevitably perform that which He promises. Abram could have asked for no greater assurance and, indeed, he moves out in faith simply on the basis of God's promise. But in a further display of His grace, God moves to embody His promises in the framework of a covenant. The covenant could not make God's word more sure, but it could make Abram more sure. The writer to the Hebrews captures the scale of God's kindness as he highlights God's motive to show more abundantly the immutability of His promise. To convey this, God once again enters into covenant with man, formally and legally committing Himself to the accomplishment of His promises.

As a number of scholars have pointed out, the covenant that God made with Abram closely resembles surviving covenants of royal grant from the ancient Near East. These promissory covenants were the legal instruments by which kings granted possession of lands to their vassals. They were marked by the monarch's unconditional commitment and invoked curses upon any who impinged upon the possession granted. This fact tends to emphasise the display of God's grace in His covenant. To give Abram the utmost possible assurance, He constructs His covenant with Abram in a way that echoes – though it ultimately transcends – contemporary legal practice. Abram's familiarity with prevailing custom would have brought forcefully before him the full significance of what God was doing, and the true implications of His covenant commitment.

The making of this covenant – the Abrahamic covenant – takes us first of all to Genesis 15. This passage demonstrates Abram's need of further confirmation of the promises he had received. The promise of a posterity, of a seed, features first. God addresses it first as the concern that was uppermost in Abram's mind, that came spilling out in response to God's words of assurance.

> After these things the word of the Lord came unto Abram in a vision, saying, Fear not, Abram: I am thy shield, and thy exceeding great reward. And Abram said, Lord God, what wilt Thou give Me, seeing I go childless, and the steward of my house is this Eliezer of Damascus? And, behold, the word of the Lord came unto him, saying, This shall not be thine heir; but he that shall come forth out of thine own bowels shall be thine heir. And he brought him forth abroad, and said, Look now toward heaven, and tell the stars, if thou be able to number them: and He said unto him, So shall thy seed be. And he believed in the Lord; and He counted it to him for righteousness (Gen. 15:1–6).

In response to Abram's question, God elaborates upon the promise of a seed given in chapter 12. Abram learns that, against his expectations, and against biological probability, God's promise would not be fulfilled by proxy but in his own descendants.

God then addresses another aspect of His promises, the possession of the land:

> And he said unto him, I am the Lord that brought thee out of Ur of the Chaldees, to give thee this land to inherit it. And he said, Lord God, whereby shall I know that I shall inherit it? (vv. 7–8).

Abram's question was by no means a pointless one. Genesis 12:6, which immediately follows the account of

Abram's departure from Haran and his arrival in Canaan, contains the bald, but significant statement that 'the Canaanite was then in the land'. Notwithstanding Abram's experience of military victory in Genesis 14, the probability of one man claiming the land that was occupied by the Canaanite must have seemed even more remote than the possibility of a son. We can measure its improbability by the action that God takes to abundantly assure the heart of Abram:

> And he said unto him, Take me an heifer of three years old, and a she goat of three years old, and a ram of three years old, and a turtledove, and a young pigeon. And he took unto him all these, and divided them in the midst, and laid each piece one against another: but the birds divided he not. And when the fowls came down upon the carcasses, Abram drove them away (Gen. 15:9–11).

These strange commands are to be understood in the context of the procedure that surrounded the 'cutting of a covenant'.* In contemporary society, one of the ways in which a covenant could be solemnised involved the killing and the cutting of an animal or animals. Both parties to the covenant would then walk between those parts. The precise meaning of this ritual is the subject of some debate, but there is a consensus that the parties were making a declaration to the effect that a breach of covenant on their part would justly merit the fate that the beasts had met. In effect, they were saying 'if I break this covenant, may I be divided in pieces like these animals.' In the formalising of the covenant with Abram,

---

* This is the literal meaning of the term usually translated as 'make' or 'establish' a covenant (See, for example, Gen. 15:18; Gen. 21:27, 32; Gen. 26:28; Gen. 31:44; Exod. 23:32; Exod. 34:10, 12, 15). The same term is used in relation to the cutting of circumcision (Ex. 4:25), and of the cutting off of the uncircumcised male from his people (Gen. 17:14).

God was entering into the prevailing norms of covenant. Abram seems to have understood this, for, as we can tell from the narrative, he did not need to be instructed to guard the carcasses and to wait for God to move.

The task of warding off the large and voracious birds of prey that would have gathered to devour the carcasses cannot but have been an arduous one. As the day drew to an end, Abram fell into a 'deep sleep'. This sleep was not simply the outcome of his exertions. The expression translated 'deep sleep' occurs on six other occasions (Gen. 2:21; 1 Sam. 26:12; Job 4:13; Job 33:15; Prov. 19:15. Isa. 29:10) in the Old Testament, and on three of those occasions explicitly refers to a sleep induced by God. The first of these mentions is the deep sleep that came upon Adam as Eve was formed. Now, God is active not in Creation but in covenant, a deep sleep falls on Abram. In that sleep an acute sense of the immensity and solemnity of the events that were about to take place came upon him:

> And when the sun was going down, a deep sleep fell upon Abram; and, lo, an horror of great darkness fell upon him (v.12).

In the mysterious silence of the ensuing dusk, God spoke, reiterating and elaborating upon His promises to Abram:

> And He said unto Abram, Know of a surety that thy seed shall be a stranger in a land that is not theirs, and shall serve them; and they shall afflict them four hundred years; And also that nation, whom they shall serve, will I judge: and afterward shall they come out with great substance. And thou shalt go to thy fathers in peace; thou shalt be buried in a good old age. But in the fourth generation they shall come

> hither again: for the iniquity of the Amorites is not yet full (Gen. 15:13–16).

Then, as Abram watched, 'a smoking furnace, and a burning lamp that passed between those pieces' (v.17). As the Theophany moved amongst the dismembered carcasses of the slain animals, God was committing Himself by His immutable covenant oath to keep the promises made to Abram. In a usual bilateral covenant, both parties would have walked together among the carcasses. But Abram is a spectator here, looking on as God unilaterally takes upon Himself the commitment of His covenant.

In Genesis 17, that covenant is further developed. Renewal of the covenant follows one of the most inglorious episodes in Abram's life – his taking of Hagar, and his subsequent expulsion of both her and her son. Sarai's attempt to anticipate the fulfilment of God's promises has proved to be nothing more than a blind alley, and the source of enduring sorrow and strife to the descendants of Abram. Thirteen nerve-wracking years of Divine silence follow, but now, God speaks once again to Abram, reiterating the promises of a seed, a land, and a blessing:

> And when Abram was ninety years old and nine, the LORD appeared to Abram, and said unto him, I am the Almighty God; walk before Me, and be thou perfect. And I will make My covenant between Me and thee, and will multiply thee exceedingly. And Abram fell on his face: and God talked with him, saying, As for Me, behold, My covenant is with thee, and thou shalt be a father of many nations. Neither shall thy name any more be called Abram, but thy name shall be Abraham; for a father of many nations have I made thee. And I will make thee exceeding fruitful, and I will make nations of thee,

and kings shall come out of thee. And I will establish My covenant between Me and thee and thy seed after thee in their generations for an everlasting covenant, to be a God unto thee, and to thy seed after thee. And I will give unto thee, and to thy seed after thee, the land wherein thou art a stranger, all the land of Canaan, for an everlasting possession; and I will be their God (Gen. 17:1–8).

As in chapters 12 and 15, God begins by declaring Who He is. In chapter 15, that revelation had a particular relevance for Abram – 'I am thy shield and thy exceeding great reward'. Now, God is making a broader claim of unbounded authority and power. It is *El Shaddai*, the Almighty God, Who renews His covenant with Abram – there can be no doubt of His right to make the promises that He does, or of His ability to keep them. A grasp of Who God is was vital to Abram's faith. The years had passed, and the arrival of a son was now not just improbable but, from a natural point of view, impossible. Notwithstanding that, 'he staggered not at the promise of God through unbelief; but was strong in faith, giving glory to God; and being fully persuaded that, what he had promised, he was able also to perform' (Rom. 4:20–21). The revelation of the Almighty God fundamentally underwrote the renewal of the covenant. Abram is almost a centenarian, and Sarai just a little younger, but the keynote of this passage is a fresh start. Abraham and Sara are given new names, the covenant is renewed, and God's purpose continues serenely on, untrammelled by human frailty or failure.

The promises of God to Abraham, confirmed by the terms of the Abrahamic covenant, are the revelation that underpin the dispensation of promise. The promises made to Abraham were reiterated later in the dispensation, to Isaac (Gen. 26:24) and to Jacob (Gen.

28:14–15; Gen. 35:10–12; Gen. 46:2–4). Towards the end of the dispensation, as Joseph's life drew to a close, he, too, looked both backwards and forwards, affirming his confidence in a faithful and covenant-keeping God:

> And Joseph said unto his brethren, I die : and God will surely visit you, and bring you out of this land unto the land which he sware to Abraham, to Isaac, and to Jacob (Gen. 50:24).

Responsibility

The fact that the New Testament uses 'promise' to describe this age gives us a clear indication of the nature of the revelation given by God. It also provides a pretty clear indication of the fundamental requirement laid upon the recipients of the promise. God promised, and confirmed that promise with the covenant oath. Now it was man's responsibility to believe God's promise.

That responsibility is clearly revealed in the life of the first patriarch. 'Abraham believed God, and it was counted unto him for righteousness' (Rom. 4:3). We have already noted that he 'staggered not through unbelief' (Rom. 4:20). Such is the prototypical value of Abraham's dependence upon God that he stands out upon the page of Scripture as the father of the faithful. And, as the promise of God was renewed with the succeeding generations, they, too, were responsible to 'count Him faithful who promised' (Heb. 11:11, *Darby*), to accept by faith that God would keep His promise.

Faith was a fundamental, but not a solitary requirement. The question of the requirements placed upon the patriarchs and their progeny during the dispensation of promise requires us to consider briefly the on-going debate about the nature of the Abrahamic covenant. On a number of occasions we have described it as a unilateral or unconditional covenant. Yet, at various points, the covenant does seem to come with conditions attached. This is especially true of Genesis 17:9–16, where the covenant sign of circumcision is introduced:

> And God said unto Abraham, Thou shalt keep My covenant therefore, thou, and thy seed after thee in their generations. This is My covenant, which ye shall keep, between Me and you and thy seed after thee; Every man child among you shall be circumcised. And ye shall circumcise the flesh of your foreskin; and it shall be a token of the covenant betwixt me and you. And he that is eight days old shall be circumcised among you, every man child in your generations, he that is born in the house, or bought with money of any stranger, which is not of thy seed. He that is born in thy house, and he that is bought with thy money, must needs be circumcised: and my covenant shall be in your flesh for an everlasting covenant. And the uncircumcised man child whose flesh of his foreskin is not circumcised, that soul shall be cut off from his people; he hath broken My covenant. And God said unto Abraham, As for Sarai thy wife, thou shalt not call her name Sarai, but Sarah shall her name be. And I will bless her, and give thee a son also of her: yea, I will bless her, and she shall be a mother of nations; kings of people shall be of her (vv. 9–16).

Over against this passage must be placed the fact that God walked alone through the animals, and His description of the covenant as everlasting (v.13). In addition, it is suggestive that the covenant is made as Abram is in 'a deep sleep', a spectator of the action, but not a participant in it.

Some commentators have circumnavigated this difficulty by suggesting that the circumcision covenant of Genesis 17:9–13 is separate and distinct from God's earlier – and unconditional – covenant. This reading is difficult to sustain. Scripture always speaks of God's covenant with Abraham in the singular, and the promises made in Genesis 17:9–13 are not new promises, but a recapitulation of God's earlier commitment.

Another, and perhaps more helpful, explanation suggests that the Abrahamic covenant is, indeed, unconditional, but that conditions do apply to participation in the covenant. This sounds like a rather tricky distinction, but it does accord well with God's solemn edict that the uncircumcised male would 'be cut off from his people' (v.14).

In any case, it is clear that circumcision, the external sign of covenant relationship with God, was a requirement in this dispensation. God was dealing in a distinct way with a single family, and He required them to be marked out as different from all the nations round about.

Those nations also had a requirement laid upon them in the dispensation of promise. In this age, God was dealing uniquely, but not exclusively with Israel. He had not forgotten the other nations. Their responsibility was connected with their response to God's chosen people. In Genesis 12 God had promised Abraham that those that blessed him would be blessed, and those that cursed him would be cursed. It is important to note that the translation here implies a stronger parallel than actually exists. Two different words are translated by 'curse'. The first might better be translated 'disdain'. Thus, God's curse would not just come upon those who cursed Abraham and his descendants, but upon those who despised them, or who regarded them with disdain.

It could be urged that this statement can hardly be regarded as a dispensational responsibility laid upon the nations as it was never revealed directly to them. This contention is not without merit, but against it must be placed the record of heathen nations and heathen rulers who came into contact with the patriarchs and who realised and acknowledged that here was a people under the protection of the Most High God. Amongst others, Abimilech, Laban, and Pharaoh would all come to realise the unique status of God's chosen people.

Rebellion

It is solemn to notice that the patriarchs and their progeny demonstrated failure in relation to each of the responsibilities laid upon them. It is also sad to observe how soon this failure manifested itself. The New Testament lauds the faith of Abraham, and we cannot but admire his dependence on God and His Word in the face of apparently overwhelming obstacles. Moreover, our knowledge of a persistent shortage of faith in our own lives, in matters that pale into insignificance by comparison with the great issues that Abraham faced, ought to make us very diffident about being too freely critical of the occasions when Abraham's faith faltered. However, Scripture does not disguise Abraham's failures of faith, and they do form an important part of the story of this dispensation of promise. They have added value for us if they challenge us to look at our own lives and to recognise the weakness of our own faith. Abraham's trip to Egypt, so soon after God had commanded him to sojourn in the land of Canaan was one of these occasions. It was compounded by the deception that he practised in Egypt, which betrayed a failure to depend upon God's promise to protect Abraham and to preserve his seed. The sordid episode with Hagar, though suggested by Sarai, was a further lapse in Abraham's faith, a doomed recourse to human expedients, rather than a faithful waiting upon God.

It is searching to note that these failures of a father and a grandfather were repeated by a son and a grandson. Isaac, too, left the land, and set his steps Egypt-ward, until God spoke directly to him. Like Abraham, he practised deceit that placed his wife in harm's way. And his determination to bless the first-born Esau, in spite of what God had revealed, demonstrated a lack of faith. At the same time, crafty Jacob's cunning plot to seize the birthright displays his failure to wait for God's time and to rely upon God's ways.

The pattern of failure in faith runs through the dispensation of promise. Notwithstanding the promises God had given, and the covenant by which He had confirmed them, the patriarchs – in difficult circumstances that explain but do not excuse their disbelief – failed simply to take God at His word. And that failure was echoed in the nation that sprang from them.

The ultimate failure of faith in the dispensation of promise took place, I want to suggest, at Kadesh-Barnea, when the Israelites, hearing of giants and of walled cities, refused to go forward in obedience to God's command and in dependence on God's promise. Demonstrating their 'evil heart of unbelief' (Heb. 3:12), they provoked, displeased, and angered God, and became the objects of His judgemental wrath.

The obvious objection to this suggestion is the fact that when the events at Kadesh-Barnea took place, the dispensation of Law had already commenced. And that is undeniably true. However, as we shall see, it is not always the case that one dispensation ends and another begins immediately. In the case of the later dispensations in particular, there is sometimes a degree of overlap and transition. In addition, as Hebrews 4 makes very clear, the failure of the nation at the border of the land was not a failure to keep the Law. Rather, it was a failure of faith, a failure to believe the promise of God.

Along with this fundamental failure come other consequent and subsidiary failures. As we have seen, God's wish was that the patriarchs remain in the land. Yet, throughout the dispensation, whenever the going got tough, the road to Egypt proved an attractive option. And the difficulty was not just that the patriarchs went towards Egypt. They also demonstrated a tendency to settle there. So, while Joseph assured his brothers that God meant his Egyptian captivity for good, and while God arranged events so that Egypt would protect the Israelites from famine, it was not His intention that they should settle there. Joseph's understanding of this is vividly portrayed in his instructions concerning his body. By contrast, the Israelites as a whole were in no hurry to leave, and it was only when oppression shook them loose that they could tear themselves from the fleshpots of Egypt.

It is noteworthy that the one requirement which did not fall into widespread neglect among the Israelites, was the external requirement of circumcision. Moses failed in this regard, requiring Zipporah to take matters into her own hands (Exod. 4:24–25), but even in Egypt, Israel had been faithful in discharging this obligation:

> At that time the LORD said unto Joshua, Make thee sharp knives, and circumcise again the children of Israel the second time. And Joshua made him sharp knives, and circumcised the children of Israel at the hill of the foreskins. And this is the cause why Joshua did circumcise: All the people that came out of Egypt, that were males, even all the men of war, died in the wilderness by the way, after they came out of Egypt. Now all the people that came out were circumcised: but all the people that were born in the wilderness by the way as they came forth out of Egypt, them they had not circumcised (Josh. 5:2–5).

It is striking that, in spite of the failure of the children of Israel to meet the inward requirements of the revelation that they had received, they did continue to practice circumcision. It is not difficult here to see traces of the attitude displayed by the Jews of our Lord's day, who insisted on external correctness, but were in heart far from God. It was right for the children of Israel to circumcise their children, but the external sign, by itself, could not compensate for the disbelief and departure of their hearts.

Retribution

Many commentators identify the oppression of the children of Israel under the whips of their Egyptian taskmasters as the culminating judgement of the dispensation of promise. Beyond question, this oppression, which had been foretold to Abraham by God, was harsh and unpleasant. As we have seen, it was also a crucial element in the process of shaking the Israelites from their Egyptian settlement. Indeed, it is remarkable that, in spite of the ardours of their experience, they were so quick to look back on Egypt with nostalgia.

If, however, we accept that the full failure of the Israelites to accept the promises of God finds its expression at Kadesh-Barnea, we must revise our views about judgement in this dispensation somewhat. In this connection, it is noteworthy that, while Scripture does not explicitly refer to slavery in Egypt as judgement, it is very clear, from both Old and New Testaments, that the wilderness wanderings of the Israelites were a judgement from a God who was not well-pleased by the unbelief of His people:

> For the children of Israel walked forty years in the wilderness, till all the people that were men of war,

> which came out of Egypt, were consumed, because they obeyed not the voice of the LORD: unto whom the LORD sware that He would not shew them the land, which the LORD sware unto their fathers that He would give us, a land that floweth with milk and honey (Josh. 5:6).
>
> As the Holy Ghost saith, To day if ye will hear His voice, harden not your hearts, as in the provocation, in the day of temptation in the wilderness: when your fathers tempted Me, proved Me, and saw My works forty years. Wherefore I was grieved with that generation, and said, they do alway err in their heart; and they have not known My ways. So I sware in my wrath, they shall not enter into My rest. (Heb. 3:8–11).

For thirty-nine wasted years they wandered, and as they travelled they marked their pathway with the bones of those who fell in death beneath the judgement of God. Virtually a whole generation died without ever entering the land that they had been promised and to which they were once so close.

Judgement in the dispensation of promise did not fall only on the Israelites. Egypt also knew the severity of God's wrath. In the plagues, in the death of the firstborn, and in the destruction of the armed might of her army and her chariots, Pharaoh and his people learned the cost of disdaining, detaining, and of damaging the people of God.

The dispensation of promise is replete with lessons for us to learn, and with practical applications to our lives. In the lives of the patriarchs, in their failures and triumphs, their advances and regresses, we see vividly portrayed the conditions of our own lives. In their encounters with God we learn, with them, of His character and His purposes. And we learn, above all, of the paralysing, impoverishing power of disbelief. We see the cost of failure to take God at His word. The writer to the Hebrews had no doubt that this was the most important lesson that the dispensation has to teach us:

> Take heed, brethren, lest there be in any of you an evil heart of unbelief, in departing from the living God (Heb. 3:12).

> Let us therefore fear, lest, a promise being left us of entering into His rest, any of you should seem to come short of it (Heb. 4:1).

We are accustomed ruefully to acknowledge our lack of faith, but we seldom take it as seriously as we should. Let us grasp the truth that our God is a God of His Word, and that our disbelief not only robs us of the wealth that He has for us, it also robs Him of His glory, and His joy in His people.

God made great promises to the patriarchs, and those immutable and irrevocable promises will yet be fulfilled. We have 'a better covenant, which was established upon better promises' (Heb. 8:6). God has 'given unto us exceeding great and precious promises' (2 Pet. 1:4). Let us lay hold upon them, enjoy them, and enter into them, knowing with assurance that 'what He [has] promised, he [is] able also to perform' (Rom. 4:21).

Chapter 11

The Dispensation of Law

AS WE SURVEY the history of the world presented to us in Scripture, it is striking how many significant events take place on mountain tops. It is as though God has chosen elevated locations in order to emphasise and underline the significance of the events that take place there. Already, we have stood with Noah on Mount Ararat, surveying the wonder of the new world. Before the story of earth's history draws to a close, we will have scaled Calvary, and surveyed the wondrous cross and its still more wondrous sacrifice. We will ascend to the top of 'Mount Zion, on the sides of the north, the city of the great king' (Ps. 48:2) and from its vantage observe with joy the splendour of the millennial kingdom. But now, we come to a different mountain, 'the mount that burned with fire' (Heb. 12:18). This mountain is associated not with a cleansed Creation, with Christ and His cross, nor with a crowned king. Here, on Mount Sinai, our interest is focused on God's covenant and God's commandment. The importance of these events is attested, not just by the elevation of the location, but by the Divine pyrotechnics that attend. God would have us to be in no doubt concerning the earth-shaking, epoch-making, and history-shaping importance of the commencement of a new nation, the inauguration of a new dispensation, and the ratification of a new covenant.

REVELATION

We can usefully begin this subject by noticing that, as with the dispensations of human government and promise, God embodies the dispensational revelation in the framework of a covenant. However, we must also carefully observe the contrast between those preceding covenants and the Mosaic covenant now offered to the nation of Israel. We have noticed that the earlier covenants were unilateral, unconditional, and everlasting. We have seen how they are modelled, to some extent, on ancient Near-Eastern covenants of grant, and that they bind an Almighty God in solemn commitment to the planet, and to the patriarchs. Now, though, we find ourselves dealing with a rather different sort of covenant.

The Mosaic covenant resembles another type of ancient covenant. Known as an obligatory covenant (or, sometimes, as a suzerain covenant), these were made between a suzerain (a sort of super-king) and inferior vassal kings. They had essentially three parts. Firstly, they contained commitments made by the suzerain. Unlike those embodied in a covenant of grant, however, these commitments were not absolute – they came with conditions attached. Failure to meet those conditions would not just free the king from his commitments; it would have negative implications embodied in the curses of the covenant.

It is obvious that the terms of the Mosaic covenant closely accord with this outline. In it, God made three mighty commitments to the new-fledged nation. He laid conditions on that nation, that fall, likewise, into three categories. Finally, the revelation concluded with the pronouncement of a series of solemn curses upon those who failed to keep the requirements of God's covenant.

In Exodus 19, God initiates His covenant. In keeping with the precedent of His covenant with Abram, and in accordance with the expected format of a covenant, He commences with a statement of His greatness, and of His achievements on behalf of Israel. This account of His past dealings with the nation provides the basis upon which He outlines the three great commitments that He was prepared to make to the nation of Israel:

> And Moses went up unto God, and the LORD called unto him out of the mountain, saying, Thus shalt thou say to the house of Jacob, and tell the children of Israel; ye have seen what I did unto the Egyptians, and how I bare you on eagles' wings, and brought you unto Myself. Now therefore, if ye will obey My voice indeed, and keep My covenant, then ye shall be a peculiar treasure unto Me above all people: for all the earth is Mine: and ye shall be unto Me a kingdom of priests, and an holy nation. These are the words which thou shalt speak unto the children of Israel (vv. 3–6).

Israel was about to begin its existence as a nation, and God reveals the special plans that He has for that nation. The nation can be God's peculiar treasure; it can be a kingdom of priests, and an holy nation. God is declaring to the Israelites His willingness to bestow these privileged offices upon them. His ownership of all the earth asserts His authority to grant these blessings, and their history assures them that the God Who is willing is also able. But even at the first making of it, God's promise is conditioned upon the nation obeying His voice and keeping His covenant.

The implications of obeying God's voice and keeping God's covenant are elaborated upon in the chapters that follow. God will instruct Moses concerning His standards. The Law given will impact upon all areas of national life, and will address moral and ethical, as well as religious issues. Detailed instructions will also be given concerning God's sanctuary; and God emphasises to Moses his responsibility to make it after the pattern showed to him in the mount (Exod. 25:9, 40; Acts 7:44; Heb. 8:5). God will also outline the service that He requires of His covenant people – the order of the priesthood and of offerings, the responsibility to tithe, the annual cycle of the feasts of Jehovah. These requirements would touch every aspect of the Israelite's life. Individually and collectively; socially, economically, and spiritually, their lives would be shaped by their effort to obey the voice of God, and to keep the terms of His covenant.

Failure to discharge their covenant responsibilities would have severe consequences. It would not just be that the nation would lose out of their promised blessing – though that by itself would be bad enough. Rather, the covenant curses imposed penalties for a failure to obey God's word, and keep His covenant. So, for example, curses can be found in the Ten Commandments:

> Thou shalt not bow down thyself to them, nor serve them: for I the LORD thy God am a jealous God, visiting the iniquity of the fathers upon the children unto the third and fourth generation of them that hate me (Exod. 20:5).

> Thou shalt not take the name of the LORD thy God in vain; for the Lord will not hold him guiltless that taketh His name in vain (Exod. 20:7).

More comprehensively, Leviticus 26 and Deuteronomy 27–28, both of which contain restatements of the Mosaic covenant, outline a terrifying series of sanctions that God would visit upon His unfaithful people. The passages need to be read in their entirety, but even in the following brief quotations, the seriousness of failure, and the severity of its judgement are starkly displayed:

> But if ye will not hearken unto Me, and will not do all these commandments; and if ye shall despise My statutes, or if your soul abhor My judgments, so that ye will not do all My commandments, but that ye break My covenant: I also will do this unto you; I will even appoint over you terror, consumption, and the burning ague, that shall consume the eyes, and cause sorrow of heart: and ye shall sow your seed in vain, for your enemies shall eat it. And I will set My face against you, and ye shall be slain before your enemies: they that hate you shall reign over you; and ye shall flee when none pursueth you (Lev. 26:14–17).

> But it shall come to pass, if thou wilt not hearken unto the voice of the LORD thy God, to observe to do all His commandments and His statutes which I command thee this day; that all these curses shall come upon thee, and overtake thee: Cursed shalt thou be in the city, and cursed shalt thou be in the field. Cursed shall be thy basket and thy store. Cursed shall be the fruit of thy body, and the fruit of thy land, the increase of thy kine, and the flocks of thy sheep. Cursed shalt thou be when thou comest in, and cursed shalt thou be when thou goest out. The LORD shall send upon thee cursing, vexation, and rebuke, in all that thou settest thine hand unto for to do, until thou be destroyed, and until thou perish quickly; because of the wickedness of thy doings, whereby thou hast forsaken Me (Deut. 28:15–20).

Such were the terms of the Mosaic covenant or, to use the synonymous term favoured by the Apostle Paul, of the Law. The revelation of this Law, in all its aspects would furnish the basis for God's dealings with His people during the course of the dispensation of Law.

In addition to thinking of the content of that revelation, it is worthwhile to think a little about the characteristics of the Law. To understand these, we need to turn to those Scriptures in our New Testament that explain for us the true status and significance of the revelation given to Moses.

Firstly, the Law is perfect. Given by God, it could not be otherwise. Paul reminded his Roman readers that 'the law is holy, and the commandment holy, and just, and good' (Rom. 7:12). It was perfect intrinsically, and in its effect. To be sure, its terms were strict and exacting. And yet, God did not give His people the Law in order that He might punish them. The standards of God, revealed in the Law, are no mere harsh and arbitrary set of rules imposed at the whim of a distant and unloving God. The Law reveals the righteousness of God, but it also establishes a code of behaviour that is good for human beings. God stressed this point in Deuteronomy 32:

> And he said unto them, Set your hearts unto all the words which I testify among you this day, which ye shall command your children to observe to do, all the words of this law. For it is not a vain thing for you; because it is your life: and through this thing ye shall prolong your days in the land, whither ye go over Jordan to possess it (vv. 46–47).

The Law of God was the life of His people, and keeping it would not only have resulted in the dispensing of promised Divine blessing, it would also have ensured a society based upon solid principles designed for the prosperity and blessing of humanity by the God Who designed and made them. History abundantly confirms this. The Mosaic covenant was made particularly and specifically with Israel, but it is nonetheless true that the principles and priorities that it embodies provide a basis for prosperous nationhood that the ideologies and ideas of men have never bettered. Throughout history, it is true, there have been many who have repeated the lie of the serpent in Eden, to deny that God's way is best. Their voices have become more vociferous in recent decades, articulating a confused and confounding dogma of relativism. We should be careful that they do not cause us to lose sight of the fact that the Law embodies sound moral principles, which express the character of God, and which are meaningless without Him. Let us thank God that the razor edge of His two-edged sword still has the power to cut away the fluff of relativism and its accompanying moral muddle. He would not have us wallow with the contemporary world in the mire, but would set our feet upon the rock, and establish our goings. We are not under Law, but we must still value highly its revelation of the character of our God.

God is a wise Creator. He is also the supreme Teacher. In the Law He has furnished Himself with a rich variety of pictures to instruct our understandings. The details provided for the pattern of God's sanctuary and the proceedings of His service sometimes seem obscure and recondite. Yet, with the help of our New Testament we can readily grasp something of the rich array of pictorial aids that our Divine Instructor has provided for us. In the Tabernacle we see the infinite glory of Christ's person itemised and illustrated for us. In the offerings, we have the infinite fulness of His work of sacrifice laid in order before us, allowing us to appreciate the richness of its complexity. In the ritual and ceremony of the feasts of Jehovah, the prophetic programme of God is summarised and vividly enacted. So richly does the Law illustrate and illuminate our own dispensation, it would be impossible to conceive what the New Testament would look like if it were shorn of the pictures limned by the Divine Artist in the giving of the Law.

In this way, we might justly describe the Law as pedagogic. But it is a different aspect of the Law's utility that Paul has in mind when he states that 'the Law was our schoolmaster [lit. pedagogue] to bring us to Christ' (Gal. 3:24). In this passage, Paul stresses the inability of the Law to provide salvation.

It comes as something of a shock to realise that the Law, given by God and communicated by angels, is powerless to save, powerless to justify, and powerless to deliver. It is important to understand that the Law was never intended to provide salvation. It was given to a people already redeemed from Egypt. It was not even given as the means of meriting entry to the land – we have already seen that Israel entered the land on the basis of the promises embodied in the Abrahamic covenant. Instead, as Leviticus 32 and Deuteronomy 32 and a host of other passages besides make clear, the Law was given to regulate the lives of those who were already redeemed and who were living in the land. Justification, in this as in every dispensation, was by faith alone.

The Law articulated a perfect standard. But it did not furnish any ability to assist the individual in meeting that standard. It was powerless, not because it was in itself deficient or flawed, but it was 'weak through the flesh' (Rom. 8:3). Its demands were so stringent, its perfection so austere that, far from removing the guilt of sin, it emphasised it, making its true heinousness and horror more clearly to appear. In light of this, how grateful ought we to be that we live in the second half of the great contrast described by the writer to the Hebrews:

> For ye are not come unto the mount that might be touched, and that burned with fire, nor unto

blackness, and darkness, and tempest, and the sound of a trumpet, and the voice of words; which voice they that heard intreated that the word should not be spoken to them any more: (for they could not endure that which was commanded, And if so much as a beast touch the mountain, it shall be stoned, or thrust through with a dart: and so terrible was the sight, that Moses said, I exceedingly fear and quake). But ye are come unto mount Sion, and unto the city of the living God, the heavenly Jerusalem, and to an innumerable company of angels, to the general assembly and church of the firstborn, which are written in heaven, and to God the Judge of all, and to the spirits of just men made perfect, and to Jesus the mediator of the new covenant, and to the blood of sprinkling, that speaketh better things than that of Abel (Heb. 12:18–24).

RESPONSIBILITY

God's words to Moses in Exodus 19 sum up, in a phrase, the responsibility of the nation of Israel under the Mosaic covenant. They were to obey His voice. In this passage, as in many others relating to the giving of the Law, there is a clear focus upon the fact of revelation, and the responsibility that it brought. This sense is echoed almost immediately in the nation's response to God's offer:

> And Moses came and called for the elders of the people, and laid before their faces all these words which the Lord commanded him. And all the people answered together, and said, All that the LORD hath spoken we will do. And Moses returned the words of the people unto the LORD (Exod. 19:7–8).

The nation's most vital responsibility in the dispensation of Law was to hear and obey the word of God. As we read through the revelation unfolded in the following chapters, we might well question whether Israel had any understanding of what it was they had so unanimously committed themselves to at Sinai. The Law was so detailed, so precise, it covered in such detail the gamut of private and public life, its requirements were so demanding that it is difficult to read them without quailing, without an overwhelming awareness of weakness and failure.

It is, however, important to remember that the revelation given to Moses included the sacrificial order as well as the commandments. The commandments, in their varying sections, and their intricate detail emphatically revealed the righteousness of God. They embodied a standard of perfection to which the Israelites could not attain. By contrast, the sacrifices revealed the grace of God. In them, provision is made for every sin and failure. In their variety they declare the fulness of God's provision, accessible to the poorest, and available to the most important. As we read the details of the sin and trespass offerings, especially, we realise that everyone needed a sacrifice and that no one was left without one.

Israel, therefore, was responsible to keep the Law, to obey God's commandments in all their diversity. But when they failed, as inevitably they would, they were responsible to use the gracious means that God had provided, to bring their sacrifice, confess their sin, and receive God's forgiveness.

Rebellion

In each of the dispensations considered so far we have seen the inevitability of human failure. In none of them, however, has that failure been so immediate and so abject as in the dispensation of Law. The nation's commitment to obey God had scarcely died on their lips, the Law was still in the process of being given, when they debased themselves in the idolatrous worship of the golden calf. Their failure was patent. They had not broken one of the minor provisions of the Law, but its very first and primary precept:

> I am the Lord thy God, which have brought thee out of the land of Egypt, out of the house of bondage. Thou shalt have no other gods before Me (Exod. 20:2–3).

And the prohibition was explicitly repeated as God spoke again to Moses on behalf of the people:

> And the LORD said unto Moses, Thus thou shalt say unto the children of Israel, Ye have seen that I have talked with you from heaven. Ye shall not make with Me gods of silver, neither shall ye make unto you gods of gold (Exod. 20:22–23).

In spite of the clarity and emphasis of this prohibition, and in spite of the people's recognition of the awful majesty of God, they were quick to forget Who God was, and what He had done. Their words to Aaron were a dreadful denial of the revelation with which God had begun the Ten Commandments:

> And when the people saw that Moses delayed to come down out of the mount, the people gathered themselves together unto Aaron, and said unto him, Up, make us gods, which shall go before us; for as for this Moses, the man that brought us up out of the land of Egypt, we wot not what is become of him (Exod. 32:1).

Not only did they disregard God's deliverance in the past, they disbelieved His promise for the future. God had given them a remarkable promise of guidance and of security:

> Behold, I send an Angel before thee, to keep thee in the way, and to bring thee into the place which I have prepared. Beware of him, and obey his voice, provoke him not; for he will not pardon your transgressions: for My name is in him. But if thou shalt indeed obey his voice, and do all that I speak; then I will be an enemy unto thine enemies, and an adversary unto thine adversaries. For Mine Angel shall go before thee, and bring thee in unto the Amorites, and the Hittites, and the Perizzites, and the Canaanites, the Hivites, and the Jebusites: and I will cut them off (Exod. 23:20–23).

Now this miraculous and remarkable provision was disdained. Rather than worship and trust the living God, the nation prostrated themselves before an inanimate representation of a dumb beast, and placed their trust in it to go before them.

Tragically, this was no isolated incident, but the prototype of a pattern that would occur, time and again, in the history of the nation. Paul, writing to the Corinthians, provides a summary of the sin that marked the nation throughout its wilderness wandering:

> Moreover, brethren, I would not that ye should be ignorant, how that all our fathers were under the cloud, and all passed through the sea; and were all baptized unto Moses in the cloud and in the sea; and did all eat the same spiritual meat; and did all drink the same spiritual drink: for they drank of that spiritual Rock that followed them: and that Rock was Christ. But with many of them God was not well pleased: for they were overthrown in the wilderness. Now these things were our examples, to

the intent we should not lust after evil things, as they also lusted. Neither be ye idolaters, as were some of them; as it is written, The people sat down to eat and drink, and rose up to play. Neither let us commit fornication, as some of them committed, and fell in one day three and twenty thousand. Neither let us tempt Christ, as some of them also tempted, and were destroyed of serpents. Neither murmur ye, as some of them also murmured, and were destroyed of the destroyer. Now all these things happened unto them for ensamples: and they are written for our admonition, upon whom the ends of the world are come (1 Cor. 10:1–11).

Nor did the situation improve once Israel was in the land. Idolatry continued to be their besetting sin, and with it came all manner of spiritual and moral evil. Under the judges and the kings, as a united and a divided kingdom, the nation of Israel demonstrated an inveterate tendency to begin by breaking the first commandment, and to carry on by breaking the rest.

For that failure, as we will see, they were judged. And, for the southern kingdom at least, the judgement of God achieved something of its corrective intention. After the return from Babylon, Judah remained free of idolatry. Their greatest failure was still to come, however. It demonstrated the incorrigible perversity of the nation, and of humanity more generally. For centuries, they had worshipped false gods, recognising as divine the gods of the pagan nations round about them. But when the Son of God came, in fulfilment of prophecy, and attested by signs and wonders, the nation failed to recognise Him, and refused to worship Him. Few Scriptures are as poignant as those that speak of Israel's failure to hail her Messiah. John reminds us that 'His own' shared the failure of the world to know the One who came:

> He was in the world, and the world was made by Him, and the world knew Him not. He came unto His own, and His own received him not (Jn 1:10–11).

Towards the end of His ministry, the Lord Jesus summarised the failure of the nation to do precisely what they had undertaken to do in Exodus 19 – to heed the voice of God. Prophets, wise men, and scribes had all been sent with God's message, but the nation's heart had been hard and their ears had been stopped. Now their failure was reaching its appalling climax, and the Lord wails, not with anger, but with an almost unbearable pathos:

> O Jerusalem, Jerusalem, thou that killest the prophets, and stonest them which are sent unto thee, how often would I have gathered thy children together, even as a hen gathereth her chickens under her wings, and ye would not! Behold, your house is left unto you desolate. For I say unto you, Ye shall not see Me henceforth, till ye shall say, Blessed is He that cometh in the name of the Lord (Mt. 23:37–39).

The parable of the vineyard, in Luke 20, had foretold what would happen. As the nation had used God's servants, so they would use His Son. And, as He stood before them, battered and bleeding, attired in mocking purple and crowned with thorns, they repudiated their promised Messiah:

> They cried out, Away with Him, away with Him, crucify Him. Pilate saith unto them, Shall I crucify your King? The chief priests answered, We have no king but Caesar (Jn 19:15).

As Pilate questioned them further, the people cried together, like a ghastly inversion of the events at Sinai.

There, with one voice they had committed themselves to keep the word of the LORD. Now, as the Word Incarnate, the Son of God, stood before them, they made another solemn pact:

> Pilate saith unto them, What shall I do then with Jesus which is called Christ? They all say unto him, Let him be crucified. And the governor said, Why, what evil hath he done? But they cried out the more, saying, Let Him be crucified. When Pilate saw that he could prevail nothing, but that rather a tumult was made, he took water, and washed his hands before the multitude, saying, I am innocent of the blood of this just person: see ye to it. Then answered all the people, and said, His blood be on us, and on our children (Mt. 27:22–25).

In every preceding dispensation, human failure involved rebellion – the rejection of God's word, the overthrow of God's authority. The culminating rebellion of the dispensation of Law dwarfed all that had gone before.

So frightful was the rebellion that took place at Calvary, so heinous was man's cruelty, that we cannot but wonder that Divine judgement, immediate and awful, did not shatter Jew and Roman alike. And yet, the men who moved in malignity against the Saviour moved in the accomplishment of God's purpose. For them He prayed as He hung upon the cross. Twelve legions of angels watched in stunned silence, waiting for the Divine command. But it never came. There, in the midst of the hatred of man, the evil of his mind, and the agony of his tortures, God was moving in accordance with His 'determinate counsel and foreknowledge' (Acts 2:23) and there, 'where sin abounded, grace did much more abound' (Rom. 5:20).

> *In battle's blazing dress they stand,*
> *With armour bright, with sword in hand,*

Prepared, upon their Master's call
To sudden swoop, destroy them all—
Imperious Roman, treacherous Jew—
Their blood to wet the ground like dew.
Twelve legions waiting but to fly.
Amazed they hear the Saviour's cry,
In love most tender, tried and true,
'Forgive, they know not what they do'.

Thus must the seraphs wondering see,
Their Lord is nailed upon a tree,
Astounded hear His piteous moan,
As bone is shook from joint with bone,
See thorn-torn brow grow drenched with sweat,
As Jesus fights the war with death;
And brutish soldiers roll the dice
Beneath the suffering sacrifice.
They of His worth so little knew:
'Forgive, they know not what they do'.

And so they watch as darkness falls,
And in that darkness hear His calls,
Alone, forsaken by His God.
Is this the Everlasting Word?
And His that awful, rending cry,
Eli Lama Sabachtani?
And yet who other could it be,
Save perfect man, yet Deity,
Who prays above that wicked crew
'Forgive, they know not what they do'.

Retribution

We must wonder that swift and awful judgement did not fall on the nation at Calvary. More remarkably still, the grace of God withheld that judgement for nearly four decades.* During that time, the gospel was preached beginning at Jerusalem (Lk. 27:47), and spreading outwards to 'all Judaea, and ... Samaria, and unto the uttermost part of the earth' (Acts 1:8). As Peter spoke to the men of Jerusalem, he spoke clearly of their sin, but also offered them the opportunity of repentance:

> The God of Abraham, and of Isaac, and of Jacob, the God of our fathers, hath glorified His Son Jesus; whom ye delivered up, and denied Him in the presence of Pilate, when he was determined to let Him go. But ye denied the Holy One and the Just, and desired a murderer to be granted unto you; and killed the Prince of life, Whom God hath raised from the dead; whereof we are witnesses. ... And now, brethren, I wot that through ignorance ye did it, as did also your rulers. But those things, which God before had shewed by the mouth of all His prophets, that Christ should suffer, He hath so fulfilled. Repent ye therefore, and be converted, that your sins may be blotted out, when the times of refreshing shall come from the presence of the Lord; and He shall send Jesus Christ, Which before was preached unto you: Whom the heaven must receive until the times of restitution of all things, which God hath spoken by the mouth of all His holy prophets since the world began (Acts 3:13–21).

But even this display of grace was insufficient to soften the heart and pierce the conscience of the nation. Having rejected the Lord, they also rejected His servants (Jn 15:20–21). As the gospel was preached, throughout the

---

* The identity of the culminating judgment of the dispensation of Law is not uncontroversial. The question is discussed in detail in the following chapter. The treatment of the issue here anticipates the conclusions arrived at in that discussion.

book of Acts, the Jews rejected it, opposed its proclamation, and persecuted its believers, until, at last, the judgement of God fell.

To identify this judgement, it is helpful to turn again to Deuteronomy 28. As we have seen, this chapter outlines the blessings and the curses connected with the Mosaic covenant. It 'is *dispensational* and *national*. ... [It] takes up the question of Israel as a nation, under the government of God.'[*] It has been argued that 'a logical analysis of the chapter is almost impossible, since the final aim was not to be logical but to build up a vivid impression by presenting picture after picture until the hearer could see and feel the import of the preacher's words.'[†] It is true that the curses outlined do contain a good deal of repetition, and employ a great deal of vivid imagery. However, it is possible to trace a progression in the curses, and to identify three separate invasions and exiles.

> The LORD shall cause thee to be smitten before thine enemies: thou shalt go out one way against them, and flee seven ways before them: and shalt be removed into all the kingdoms of the earth (Deut. 28:25).

> The LORD shall bring thee, and thy king which thou shalt set over thee, unto a nation which neither thou nor thy fathers have known; and there shalt thou serve other gods, wood and stone. And thou shalt become an astonishment, a proverb, and a byword, among all nations whither the LORD shall lead thee. ... Thou shalt beget sons and daughters, but thou shalt not enjoy them; for they shall go into captivity (Deut. 28:36–37, 41).

---

[*] C.H. Mackintosh, *Deuteronomy*, (New York: Loiseaux Brothers, 1879),

[†] J.A. Thompson, *Deuteronomy: An Introduction and Commentary*, (London: Inter-varsity Press, 1974), 271

> The LORD shall bring a nation against thee from far, from the end of the earth, as swift as the eagle flieth; a nation whose tongue thou shalt not understand; a nation of fierce countenance, which shall not regard the person of the old, nor shew favour to the young: and he shall eat the fruit of thy cattle, and the fruit of thy land, until thou be destroyed: which also shall not leave thee either corn, wine, or oil, or the increase of thy kine, or flocks of thy sheep, until he have destroyed thee. And he shall besiege thee in all thy gates, until thy high and fenced walls come down, wherein thou trustedst, throughout all thy land: and he shall besiege thee in all thy gates throughout all thy land, which the LORD thy God hath given thee. And thou shalt eat the fruit of thine own body, the flesh of thy sons and of thy daughters, which the Lord thy God hath given thee, in the siege, and in the straitness, wherewith thine enemies shall distress thee (Deut. 28:49–53).

History records three significant events of attack and exile – by Assyria, by Babylon, and by Rome. Long before these events had taken place, they were foretold by God, as a stern warning of the consequences of covenant breaking.

The chapter builds towards a climax, and progressively more detail is provided concerning the judgements that would fall. The final siege, conquest, and dispersion is described in extensive detail:

> And ye shall be left few in number, whereas ye were as the stars of heaven for multitude; because thou wouldest not obey the voice of the LORD thy God. And it shall come to pass, that as the LORD rejoiced over you to do you good, and to multiply you; so the LORD will rejoice over you to destroy you, and to bring you to nought; and ye shall be plucked from

off the land whither thou goest to possess it. And the LORD shall scatter thee among all people, from the one end of the earth even unto the other; and there thou shalt serve other gods, which neither thou nor thy fathers have known, even wood and stone. And among these nations shalt thou find no ease, neither shall the sole of thy foot have rest: but the LORD shall give thee there a trembling heart, and failing of eyes, and sorrow of mind: And thy life shall hang in doubt before thee; and thou shalt fear day and night, and shalt have none assurance of thy life: In the morning thou shalt say, Would God it were even! and at even thou shalt say, Would God it were morning! for the fear of thine heart wherewith thou shalt fear, and for the sight of thine eyes which thou shalt see. And the LORD shall bring thee into Egypt again with ships, by the way whereof I spake unto thee, Thou shalt see it no more again: and there ye shall be sold unto your enemies for bondmen and bondwomen, and no man shall buy you (Deut. 28:62–68).

It is striking – though not, of course, surprising – that the events surrounding the fall of Jerusalem to the Roman forces in AD 70 correspond so closely to the description.

Even by the robust standards of ancient war, the horror of the siege of Jerusalem stands out. Our knowledge of these events comes principally from the writings of Flavius Josephus, a Jewish historian who was with the Romans at Jerusalem. A veteran of the first Roman-Jewish war, and a survivor of the siege and mass suicide at Yodfat, his account nonetheless reverberates with the unprecedented and unparalleled horror of the events that he witnessed and recorded.

The inhabitants of Jerusalem were already suffering before the arrival of Titus' legions. Three rival rulers struggled for control of the city, and their struggles led to the widespread violence. Even as Titus' four legions surrounded the city, they were unable to unite against the common enemy. Cut off from sources of food and water, famine began to grip the city, compounded by the thousands of Passover pilgrims whose presence swelled the population of Jerusalem. The appalling events predicted in Deuteronomy took place as all order broke down. Men tortured and killed each other in their quest for food. Josephus reports not just cannibalism, but mothers eating their own young. All the while, the Roman bombardment of the city continued, as the scorpions and catapults launched bolts and boulders into the city streets. Below, at the base of the walls, the vast battering rams pounded incessantly.

Some sought to flee the violence and despair of the city, but they found little relief. Some of those fleeing tried to take their savings with them, by swallowing gold coins and jewels. The Romans, realising this, began to eviscerate all captured escapees, searching their intestines for hidden treasure. Others 'were first whipped, and then tormented with all sorts of tortures, before they died, and were then crucified before the wall of the city'*, in an effort to horrify its inhabitants into surrender. Over five hundred a day died like this, a number 'so great, that room was wanting for the crosses, and crosses wanting for the bodies'. The Roman soldiers relieved the tedium of the torture by crucifying their victims in grotesque positions.

And this was still the prelude. As the city's three walls fell, the invaders and defenders fought hand to hand, from street to street. Eventually, the impregnable Antonia fortress fell, and the remaining defenders fell

---

* Flavius Josephus, *The Jewish Wars*, trans. William Whiston, BJ5.446, (available on-line at http://perseus.uchicago.edu/

back on the Temple Mount and the upper city. Titus had not planned the destruction of the Temple. Indeed, he had given orders to his soldiers that this magnificent edifice was to be preserved. God, however, had decreed that there should 'not be left one stone upon another, that shall not be thrown down' (Mt. 24:2; Mk 13:2). And so it was. A Roman soldier threw a burning brand into the Temple. On the anniversary of the destruction of the Temple by Nebuchadnezzar, Herod's magnificent construction went up in flames, signalling a free-for-all for looting legionaries. As the gold melted it ran between the stones of the Temple, and as the soldiers sought it they dismantled it stone by stone, until Christ's prophecy was fulfilled. The fire spread beyond the Temple, and the fight was all but over.

No one knows how many died during the siege of Jerusalem. Tacitus gives a figure of 600,000 and Josephus says that over a million died. Tens of thousands more were sold into slavery, just as Deuteronomy had predicted. The Temple was destroyed, all the priests killed, and Judaism would never be the same again. Ever since, their experience has been the tragedy of exile so movingly described by Moses.

It is worth pausing to reflect on the dispensational significance of this event. Only a generation earlier, a Passover crowd in Jerusalem had cried 'His blood be on us, and on our children' (Mt. 27:25). Those words had taken on a concrete and horrific reality. Throughout the period covered by the book of Acts, the focus of Divine activity had increasingly shifted from the Jews to the Gentiles. The nation had rejected the overtures of the gospel, had refused to repent and accept her Messiah. Now, her house was, in truth, left unto her desolate (Mt. 23:38; Lk. 13:35), at first a rubbish heap, and then a pagan shrine, but consistently forbidden to the nation that had failed so signally to do all that the Lord said unto them.

It can give us no pleasure to contemplate the judgement of the Jews. Nor can their failure excuse the grievous history of anti-Semitism that has so besmirched the history of the world. As we think of their experience, we learn of the righteousness and fearsomeness of God. But we learn too of His grace. In His hand, the failure of the Jews brought blessing to the world:

> Have they stumbled that they should fall? God forbid: but rather through their fall salvation is come unto the Gentiles, for to provoke them to jealousy. Now if the fall of them be the riches of the world, and the diminishing of them the riches of the Gentiles; how much more their fulness? ... For if the casting away of them be the reconciling of the world, what shall the receiving of them be, but life from the dead (Rom. 11:11–12, 15).

As we contemplate the greatness of God's dispensational dealings with the world, the nation, and with us, we cannot find a more appropriate response than that which was wrung from the heart of the Apostle to the Gentiles as he traced the same Divine plan:

> O the depth of the riches both of the wisdom and knowledge of God! How unsearchable are His judgments, and His ways past finding out! For who hath known the mind of the Lord? or who hath been His counsellor? Or who hath first given to Him, and it shall be recompensed unto him again? For of Him, and through Him, and to Him, are all things: to Whom be glory for ever. Amen (Rom. 11:33–36).

Chapter 12

The Dispensation of Grace

THE DISPENSATION OF LAW commenced on the literal summit of Mount Sinai. The dispensation of Grace begins, not on a literal mountain, but in a room somewhere in Jerusalem. Notwithstanding the ordinary setting where God poured out His Spirit, and inaugurated a new dispensation, we are brought in this dispensation to the summit of a spiritual Everest. As we have journeyed towards this dispensation, we have experienced many ups and downs. We have, at times, scaled great peaks of Divine grace, but even as we have stood there, we have felt our foothold to be precarious, and known that all too soon a descent into the valley of human failure awaited us. We have, in fact, been moving through the foothills of God's purpose, and, in spite of the depth of the valleys, each peak has lifted us higher than the last, until we have arrived at the zenith of God's purpose for this world. It is as if, to change our mountaineering image for a musical, the eternal Conductor has led the orchestra of the universe through successive crescendo and diminuendo, building the volume, force, and grandeur of His theme until we arrive at the climax of His composition.

The dispensation of grace is not the last of the dispensations. But it is the period spoken of in Scripture as the consummation, the climax of the ages (1 Cor. 10:11; Heb. 9:26). It is in this unique epoch that God's eternal purposes of salvation find their ultimate achievement. It is in this age that He will find a bride for His Son, and it is during this period that He will gather an innumerable number of souls, who will populate Heaven, in the likeness of His beloved Son. All of past history has been preparatory for this age. Its patchwork, piecemeal revelations (Heb. 1:1–2), its exigencies and events (1 Cor. 10:11) have all been arranged by the mighty hand of God to set the stage for this greatest and grandest of the dispensations.

In view of the status of this age, it seems strange that we often hear it referred to as a parenthesis in the Divine programme. In grammatical terms, a parenthesis is generally used (as it is here) to set apart clauses (like this one) that are not essential to the meaning of the sentence or the construction of an argument. In fact, to speak of the dispensation of grace as a parenthesis is not the happiest choice of terminology, and it has led some critics of dispensationalism to claim that dispensationalists are guilty of under-estimating the importance and uniqueness of the Church in the plan of God. It hardly needs to be said that such critics are not only mindless of the large amounts of dispensational teaching that do precisely the reverse of what they suggest, they are also being wilfully obtuse in reading too much into the figurative use of a grammatical term. Nonetheless, describing the dispensation of grace as a mystery might, perhaps, be more Scriptural, as well as less susceptible to misinterpretation.

More important than the terminology, of course, is the truth that it is intended to convey. That truth is the fact that the details of the dispensation of grace, in particular the truth concerning the calling out, character, composition, and rapture of the Church, are not revealed in the Old Testament. As far as the writers of Old Testament Scripture were concerned, the age in which we presently find ourselves did not exist. It was concealed from their view and, just as a man may look from one mountain top to another, and never realise that a vast and populous valley lies between, they looked from the first coming of Christ to the Millennium without appreciating what lay between.

It is clear, then, that this present dispensation is not only the climax of the ages. It is also distinct in its character from all the other dispensations. It is useful to notice just a few of the ways in which it stands out from them.

Firstly, this dispensation is heavenly in its focus. In earlier dispensations, God dealt with a race, a family and a nation, and always in the context of the earth. Adam and Noah were to exercise authority over the earth, Abram was promised a portion of the earth, and the Mosaic covenant was made with an earthly nation. The primary focus of the Millennium, too, will be the rule and administration of earth. In this dispensation, God has not abandoned the earth. However, the focus of His purpose is not earthly but heavenly. The Church that Christ is building is a heavenly body, that transcends national, ethnic, and social distinctions (Gal. 2:28). The individual believer, too, is seen as seated 'in heavenly places in Christ Jesus' (Eph. 2:6), appropriating by faith a new order of existence, and a new realm of service and strife (Eph. 6:12).

Secondly, the dispensation of grace is eternal in its purpose. When Scripture speaks of the purpose of God for and concerning His own in this dispensation, it speaks of their formation 'before the foundation of the world' (Eph. 1:4; 1 Pet. 1:20). Strikingly, in John 17, Christ uses the same language concerning Himself (Jn 17:24). This contrasts with God's purpose for Israel and for the nations, which was from the foundation of the world (Mt. 25:34; Heb. 4:3). And God's plans are not only eternal in their intention; they are also eternal in their duration. Notwithstanding Israel's uniqueness amongst the nations, she, and they, will ultimately be brought to an end. Eternally the Church will be the Bride of Christ and her unique position of privilege will endure throughout all eternity.

Thirdly, the dispensation of grace is spiritual in its realm. It is spiritual in its warfare. When Israel entered the land, they faced the opposition of the Canaanites, the Hittites, the Amorites, the Hivites, the Jebusites, and a host of other euphonious enemies. By contrast, in this dispensation, 'we wrestle not against flesh and blood, but against principalities, against powers, against the rulers of the darkness of this world, against spiritual wickedness in high places' (Eph. 6:12). The Saviour identified enemies of the same sort in His promise:

> Thou art Peter, and upon this rock I will build My church; and the gates of hell shall not prevail against it (Mt. 16:18).

Such enemies are not to be faced in the power of the flesh, but in the power of the Holy Spirit.

In addition, it is spiritual in its wisdom. Paul wrote to the Corinthian believers in part to dissuade them from their love and valorisation of earthly wisdom. In doing so, he drew a stark line between the partial perishing wisdom that typifies the efforts of man's mind, and the wisdom designed by God, intended for us, and imparted by the Spirit of God:

> Howbeit we speak wisdom among them that are perfect: yet not the wisdom of this world, nor of the

princes of this world, that come to nought: But we speak the wisdom of God in a mystery, even the hidden wisdom, which God ordained before the world unto our glory: which none of the princes of this world knew: for had they known it, they would not have crucified the Lord of glory (1 Cor. 2:6–8).

In this dispensation, as we have noted in an earlier chapter, we worship in the Spirit. The magnificence of the Temple, and the order of its service have both alike passed away. We do not come to a physical place. We do not employ physical means – not animal sacrifices or musical accompaniment, the sweet smell of incense or the glow of the lampstand. Instead, we worship as a heavenly people, offering 'the sacrifice of praise to God continually, that is, the fruit of our lips giving thanks to His name' (Heb. 13:15).

We are equipped for these spiritual exercises and efforts because God has given us His Holy Spirit. On the day of Pentecost the Spirit was given. The Church, the body of Christ, was baptised in the Spirit (Acts 1:4–5; Acts 11:16). At the moment of conversion, each believer is sealed with the Spirit of Promise (Eph. 1:13), indwelt by God's Spirit (1 Cor. 6:19–20). Each New Testament church, too, is 'the temple of God' indwelt by the Holy Spirit (1 Cor. 3:17).

The dispensation of grace is, therefore, distinct from all other dispensations in its spiritual character, its heavenly focus and its eternal place in the purposes of God. We sometimes succumb to Biblical nostalgia and think how it would have been to have lived in an earlier age. But when we think like this we have lost sight of the privilege of living in this unique period, of enjoying its promises, and seeing all of history – past and future – from the clarity of its lofty perspective.

Revelation

This remarkable dispensation was inaugurated by an extraordinary revelation. The epistle to the Hebrews, as we have already seen, opens by summarising the history of revelation, and presents the contrasting grandeur of God's revelation of Himself in the one Who is intrinsically and characteristically His Son:

> God, Who at sundry times and in divers manners spake in time past unto the fathers by the prophets, hath in these last days spoken unto us by His Son, Who being the brightness of His glory, and the express image of His person, and upholding all things by the word of His power, when He had by Himself purged our sins, sat down on the right hand of the Majesty on high: being made so much better than the angels, as He hath by inheritance obtained a more excellent name than they (Heb. 1:1–4).

The scale and the significance of this are difficult for us to grasp. It is not simply the case, as it might be in a human context, that the Son resembled the Father. Rather, He was the express image of His person. All that God is was made visible in Christ, all that we will ever know of God is told forth in Him. We are amazed and wonder-struck by all that we find in the written Word of God, but that Word, while fully sufficient, is not exhaustive. There were, John tells us 'many other things' (Jn 21:25) which could have been written and were not. Those other things were all found in the perfect Son of God, and, like the hidden manna concealed within the ark (Rev. 2:17), will feed and sustain us through all eternity.

This revelation was unparalleled in its medium. It was, in addition, new in its content. Both John the

Apostle and John the Baptist stress the nature of this revelation:

> And the Word was made flesh, and dwelt among us, (and we beheld His glory, the glory as of the only begotten of the Father,) full of grace and truth (Jn 1:14).

> John bare witness of Him, and cried, saying, This was He of whom I spake, He that cometh after me is preferred before me: for He was before me. And of His fulness have all we received, and grace for grace. For the law was given by Moses, but grace and truth came by Jesus Christ. No man hath seen God at any time, the only begotten Son, which is in the bosom of the Father, He hath declared Him (Jn 1:15–18).

It is not that grace and truth were unknown before this dispensation. We have traced both through the centuries of earth's history. However, both God's grace and His truth would reach their apotheosis in this age, and in this revelation. And they would be revealed hand-in-hand. The Law emphasises truth, but not grace. Now grace is emphasised, but not by a muddying of God's standards, or at the expense of truth. In the life and death of the Lord Jesus Christ, 'mercy and truth are met together; righteousness and peace have kissed each other' (Ps. 85:10). Time and again, we see the lovely, exquisitely balanced combination. He was the One Who could say to the woman taken in adultery, 'Neither do I condemn thee: go, and sin no more' (Jn 8:11). Sin was identified, and sin was forgiven, and the cost of that forgiveness would ultimately be borne by the One Who imparted it. On the cross, He embodied the grace of God as He 'suffered, the just for the unjust' (1 Pet. 3:18). But, in every pang of His sufferings, He also epitomised the truth and the righteousness of God. He had prayed 'My

Father, if it be possible, let this cup pass from me' (Mt. 26:39), and it was Divine righteousness and Divine truth that made it impossible for His prayer to be answered.

Like the dispensations of promise and of Law, the dispensation of grace also has a covenant associated with it. This 'new covenant' was announced in Jeremiah 31:31–34, and is restated in Hebrews 8:

> But now hath He obtained a more excellent ministry, by how much also He is the mediator of a better covenant, which was established upon better promises. ... For this is the covenant that I will make with the house of Israel after those days, saith the Lord; I will put my laws into their mind, and write them in their hearts: and I will be to them a God, and they shall be to me a people: and they shall not teach every man his neighbour, and every man his brother, saying, Know the Lord: for all shall know Me, from the least to the greatest. For I will be merciful to their unrighteousness, and their sins and their iniquities will I remember no more. In that He saith, A new covenant, he hath made the first old. Now that which decayeth and waxeth old is ready to vanish away (vv. 6–13).

The new covenant is a complex subject and has caused no little controversy, not least because it applies to Israel, but also to the believers of this dispensation. Its fulfilment for Israel will take place in the Millennium, and we can therefore leave discussion of that aspect of the covenant to the next chapter. The more difficult question remains – how do we, as believers in the dispensation of grace, relate to this new covenant?

That there is a relationship would be difficult to deny. The Lord Jesus, inaugurating the Last Supper, spoke of the New Testament in His blood (Mt. 26:28; Lk. 22:20). Nor is it without significance that the same detail was included in the revelation of the Last Supper to Paul (1 Cor. 11:25). Indeed, Paul would speak of himself and his fellow servants as 'able ministers of the new testament' (2 Cor. 3:6). Moreover, as we have seen, the writer to the Hebrews describes Christ's mediatorship of the new covenant. But these passages, in themselves, hardly help us to understand how we come to have a part in a covenant made by God with Israel and Judah.

In this connection, the second chapter of the epistle to the Ephesians helps us to understand how we have entered into the enjoyment of the new covenant:

> Wherefore remember, that ye being in time past Gentiles in the flesh, who are called Uncircumcision by that which is called the Circumcision in the flesh made by hands; that at that time ye were without Christ, being aliens from the commonwealth of Israel, and strangers from the covenants of promise, having no hope, and without God in the world: but now in Christ Jesus ye who sometimes were far off are made nigh by the blood of Christ (Eph. 2:11–13).

The Gentile Ephesians were once outside of the scope of Divine purpose. Specifically, they had no place in the covenants of promise in which the Jews gloried (Rom. 9:4). But now, a great change has taken place. In Christ Jesus, and through the blood of Christ, Gentiles have been made nigh. And it is not that they have become Jews. As Paul demonstrates in the following verses, Jew and Gentile alike have been brought into 'one body', to 'one new man'; the 'middle wall of partition' has been broken down (Eph. 2:14–16). In Christ, we participate even now in the new covenant, a blessing that Israel will not enjoy until she is restored under the millennial reign of Christ.

These new covenant blessings are made good to us through the ministry of the Holy Spirit. Before His death, Christ promised His disciples the power of the Spirit to instruct and direct them:

> But the Comforter, which is the Holy Ghost, Whom the Father will send in My name, He shall teach you all things, and bring all things to your remembrance, whatsoever I have said unto you (Jn 14:26).

No doubt those apostles who were used of God in the writing down of inspired Scripture benefitted from this ministry in a unique way. Nonetheless, it was promised to all, and still it is a vital part of the ministry of the Holy Spirit to unfold to us 'the deep things of God' (1 Cor. 2:10).

Nor is this the extent of revelation in the dispensation of grace. The Ephesians were reminded that the basis for their belief was 'the foundation of the apostles and prophets, Jesus Christ himself being the chief corner stone' (Eph. 2:20). In Acts 2:42, we learn that the apostles' doctrine was of crucial importance for the early believers. And God has seen to it that the apostles' doctrine, the 'faith that was once for all delivered to the saints' (Jude 3) has been recorded for us in His Word. Adequately to survey this mighty storehouse of God's Word would be well beyond the scope of this chapter – or of this book. It is worthwhile, nonetheless, briefly to mention the relevance and importance of the mystery doctrines of the New Testament. These doctrines are not mysterious in any occult or gnostic sense. They are, simply, truths that God had previously kept concealed, but has now revealed. Depending on the commentator, as many as fourteen of these mystery doctrines have been identified – though some of these are arguably best understood as different aspects of particular doctrines. This most extensive classification lists these doctrines as follows:

Doctrinal

Mystery of the Faith – 1 Timothy 3:9
Mystery of the Gospel – Romans 16:25; Ephesians 6:19
Mystery of Jew and Gentile in one body – Ephesians 3
Mystery of the Bride – Ephesians 5:32; Revelation 19–20
Mystery of the seven stars and seven churches – Revelation 1:20
Mystery of Godliness – 1 Timothy 3:16

Dispensational

Mystery of the Kingdom of Heaven – Matthew 13
Mystery of Israel's Blindness – Romans 11:25
Mystery of the Rapture of the Church – 1 Corinthians 15:51
Mystery of His will – Ephesians 1:9
Mystery of God – Revelation 10:7

Devotional

Mystery of the indwelling Christ – Colossians 1:24–29

Diabolical

Mystery of iniquity – 2 Thessalonians 2:7
Mystery, Babylon the great – Revelation 17–18[*]

Manifestly, all of these are important truths, and each is deserving of detailed study in its own right. The point to be noted here, though, is that in this dispensation, which was concealed from God's people in the past, God has made known many significant and vital truths that were, likewise, hidden to even the greatest believers in ages that are past. This should help to reinforce and underline our sense of the uniqueness of this

---

[*] T. Ernest Wilson, *Mystery Doctrines of the New Testament: God's Sacred Secrets*, (Neptune, NJ: Loizeaux Brothers, 1975), 11–2

dispensation, and the distinctiveness of what God is doing in this, the climax of the ages.

Responsibility

The responsibility placed upon man in the dispensation of grace is, perhaps, most succinctly summarised in the words of the Great Commission. As the Saviour addressed His own, just before His departure back to Heaven, He gave them a mighty promise and a tremendous mandate:

> And Jesus came and spake unto them, saying, All power is given unto Me in heaven and in earth. Go ye therefore, and teach all nations, baptizing them in the name of the Father, and of the Son, and of the Holy Ghost: teaching them to observe all things whatsoever I have commanded you: and, lo, I am with you always, even unto the end of the world. Amen (Mt. 28:18–20).

It is precious to note that the promises of Christ's power and presence sandwich His commandment. The risen Lord was about to outline an ambitious and demanding programme that would be worldwide in its focus and millennia-long in its duration. But before He gives His disciples their task and their mandate, He identifies for them the power that will enable and assist the discharge of their weighty responsibility. And, as they felt the burden of this new role, He reassures them of His unceasing and unfailing presence. They would not be on their own, they would not need to rely on their own strength. The Saviour Who gave the responsibility also gave the resources that it required.

The responsibilities outlined in the commission can be divided into different sections. The disciples were responsible to go, to teach, and to baptise. They were to be faithful in their teaching – all things that the Saviour commanded were to be taught, the truth that He had revealed was to be preserved and perpetuated.

Those who heard the teaching of the apostles – particularly the preaching of the gospel – had a responsibility that is starkly stated in Mark's gospel: 'He that believeth and is baptized shall be saved; but he that believeth not shall be damned' (Mk 16:16). Sinners were responsible to believe the gospel, to be baptised, and to observe all things that the Lord had commanded.

Essentially, man's responsibility in the dispensation of grace is the same as it has been in every other dispensation. He is required to trust and obey: to trust God for salvation and in service, and to obey both the command of the gospel and the teachings of God's Word.

(THE TRIBULATION)

Before we attempt to understand how man has failed and will yet fail in the discharge of this responsibility, it is necessary to make a slight digression, in order to consider where the Tribulation fits in relation to the dispensations. We know, of course, where it belongs chronologically. The seven years of Tribulation commence after the Rapture (precisely how long after the Rapture is a subject for conjecture, as Scripture gives us no specific timescale). They will end with the Second Coming of Christ to earth, which will, in turn, inaugurate the Millennium. Though we can locate the period in time, identifying the dispensation to which it belongs is a more complex issue. Broadly speaking, there are three positions that have been espoused by students of Scripture. Some commentators have suggested that the Tribulation is the closing judgement of the dispensation of Law. Others suggest that it is a dispensation entire of itself. Finally, it has been suggested by some that the Tribulation is the closing judgement of the dispensation of grace.

Before embarking on a discussion of these positions, a few general points might usefully be made. Firstly, this is not an area where dogmatism is at all helpful. As is witnessed by the variety of views, and the number of commentators who manage to skate over this issue without committing to a particular position, this is not a straightforward issue. Secondly, there is a danger in allowing our position to be determined by the definitions that we bring to Scripture. There is a fine balance between deducing a definition from the evidence of Scripture, and bringing to Scripture a definition that we have devised ourselves, or that has been passed to us by our doctrinal forefathers. We need to test our definitions by Scripture, and not *vice versa*. The third point to bear well towards the front of our minds is that it is seldom useful to try to impose rigid divisions on Scripture. This has been a traditional shortcoming of dispensational teaching, which has sometimes – whether intentionally or otherwise – seemed to suggest that one dispensation ends at 12 midnight, and another begins at 12:01. As we have seen, particularly in the dispensations of promise and of Law, such a sharp discontinuity did not occur – the dispensations do overlap slightly, and there is a transitional period between them. So, for example, the 38 years in the wilderness was a transitional period (indeed, a transitional generation) between promise and Law, and the period covered by the book of the Acts, from the resurrection to AD 70 (again, a generation) is clearly transitional in character. God's programme is rich and complex beyond our imagining, and we must be careful not to be reductive or simplistic in our understanding of that programme. With these caveats lodged firmly in our minds, we will be better placed to weigh up and perhaps even to decide between the possible solutions to this conundrum.

The idea that the Tribulation closes the dispensation of Law has been espoused by a number of commentators. Lewis Chafer is perhaps the most influential and considerable of these, and is well-equipped to speak for himself:

> In determining the dispensation to which the Tribulation period belongs, it should be observed that it bears no relation to the features of this church age, nor has it the characteristics of a dispensation in itself. Though it is the consummation of Divine judgment upon all men and their institutions, it is especially Israelitish. The continuity of that Jewish age which began at Sinai is incomplete apart from the events which belong to the Great Tribulation. As stated by Daniel, the seventieth week is required for the finishing of Israel's transgression and the bringing in of everlasting righteousness (Dan. 9:24–27). The transgression to be 'finished' could be no part of this age of grace, but is rather of the preceding age. The fact that the general features which obtain in the Tribulation are similar to those principles which were peculiar to the law age is also conclusive. The sabbath is re-established (Mt. 24:20), the Temple worship is renewed – though in unbelief – (Mt. 24:15; 2 Thess. 2:4), the Old Testament kingdom-hope will again be announced (Mt. 24:14), and the legal principle of merit and reward for endurance will again obtain throughout that brief period (Mt. 24:13). Not only does the law dispensation require the yet future Tribulation period for the execution of those Divine judgements which belong to it, but, by the recognition of the sequence connecting these two

> periods of time, the continuity of purpose is preserved wherein the Messianic, earthly kingdom, which follows the Tribulation, is seen to be both the legitimate expectation and the logical consummation of the dispensation of the law. By so much it may be observed that the present unforeseen dispensation of grace is wholly parenthetical within the dispensation of the Law.*

Chafer's position is effectively articulated, and there is much about it that is attractive. However, there are a number of difficulties that must be noted.

His contention that 'The continuity of that Jewish age which began at Sinai is incomplete apart from the events which belong to the Great Tribulation' begs the question – it assumes what it is intended to prove. Daniel 9:24 refers not just to the Tribulation, but to the whole of the seventy weeks, and is worth quoting fully:

> Seventy weeks are determined upon thy people and upon thy holy city, to finish the transgression, and to make an end of sins, and to make reconciliation for iniquity, and to bring in everlasting righteousness, and to seal up the vision and prophecy, and to anoint the most Holy.

The verse outlines a comprehensive programme, which embraces much more than judgement, and, while it does prove that God is dealing with Israel during the Tribulation, it does not prove that Tribulation judgement pertains to the dispensation of Law. Nor is it necessarily accurate to say that 'the law dispensation require[s] the yet future Tribulation period for the execution of those Divine judgements which belong to

---

* Lewis Sperry Chafer, *Major Bible Themes* (available online at http://www.davidcox.com.mx/library/C/Chafer/chafer_major_bible_themes _18.htm, accessed 14 June 2012.)

it.' We have already noted that Divine judgement did fall upon Israel in AD 70, and we have observed, too, how closely the details of that judgement accorded with the curses of the Mosaic covenant. Additionally, his suggested solution simply moves this problem along, for it leaves the dispensation of grace without a culminating rebellion and a culminating judgement.

Chafer's acknowledgement that the Tribulation 'is the consummation of Divine judgment upon all men and their institutions' is important, and makes a point to which we shall return. His contention that this judgement is 'especially Israelitish' is problematic. It is true that the Tribulation – especially the second half of the seven years, or the Great Tribulation – will be a time when Israel comes under tremendous pressure. But she will suffer at the hands of man, and particularly of the Beast. The Divine judgements that are poured out in the Tribulation are international and global in their scope. God will resume His providential dealing with Israel, but His judgement will be neither exclusively nor especially for her.

It is difficult to disagree with Chafer's suggestion that 'the Messianic, earthly kingdom, which follows the Tribulation, is ... both the legitimate expectation and the logical consummation of the dispensation of the Law', but, as we shall see, the Millennium is far more than that, and accomplishes purposes more diverse and grander than simply functioning as the 'logical consummation of the dispensation of Law'. Chafer is, of course, correct in pointing out that some elements of the Mosaic system – particularly some of the Temple service and sacrifices – will resume. However, it is important to understand that the Law will not be reinstated as the principle upon which God is dealing with man. In the dispensation of conscience, God dealt with man primarily on the basis of conscience. The close of the dispensation did not remove or exterminate conscience, but it ceased to be the basis upon which God dealt with mankind. Again, the giving of the Law did not annul the promises of God (Gal. 3:17), but Promise ceased to be the distinctive dispensational principle. To say that elements of the service introduced under the Law are reinstated does not prove that we are once again in the dispensation of Law. And, in fact, mankind is not being tested on the keeping of the Law. Those who are saved in the Tribulation will not be in the same position as the righteous Israelite before Calvary. They cannot be, for Christ has 'blott[ed] out the handwriting of ordinances that was against us, which was contrary to us, and took it out of the way, nailing it to his cross' (Col. 2:15). 'Christ is the end of the Law' (Rom. 10:4), and the fundamental difficulty with this position is that it compromises this tremendous truth.

The second position – that the Tribulation constitutes a dispensation in its own right has not been, as far as I have been able to discover, articulated in print. Essentially, though, it presents a simple argument. Those who take this position suggest that the dispensation of grace ends, conterminously with the Church age, at the moment of the Rapture. They point to the distinctiveness of the way in which God is dealing with mankind during the Tribulation, particularly in relation to His resumption of dealings with Israel. However, in the quotation from Chafer above, the greatest difficulty with this dispensation is clearly stated: the Tribulation does not have 'the characteristics of a dispensation in itself'. In each of the dispensations we have noticed the same characteristics – revelation, responsibility, rebellion, and retribution – repeated. The Tribulation does not follow this pattern. There is no specific revelation – the gospel of the kingdom that will be preached in the Tribulation (Mt. 24:13) is not a fresh revelation, but a call for repentance and faith that differs from the gospel preached today primarily in the eschatological urgency imparted by the fact that 'the kingdom of God is at hand'. There is, therefore, no distinctive test for mankind in the Tribulation. As a consequence of this, the failure – the rebellion – that is judged is not distinctive to the period either. To make a dispensation of the Tribulation requires a degree of special pleading and such special pleading is usually best avoided. In addition seeing the Tribulation as a separate dispensation shares the difficulty that it leaves the dispensation of grace without a closing judgement.

The third possibility is to see the Tribulation as the culmination of the dispensation of grace. This view is not without its own difficulties. Most notably, it means that the Church age and the dispensation of grace are no longer exactly conterminous. The Church age ends at the Rapture, but, in this reading, the dispensation of grace extends beyond the Rapture for more than seven years. It is also true that the earthly focus of the Tribulation, and the fact that God begins to deal again with Israel contradict the heavenly, Church-centred character of the dispensation of grace. This is a fair and weighty criticism, but we return to our earlier point about the variety of Divine operation that takes place during the Tribulation. The period does involve a transition towards the Millennium. Much unfinished business is taken up again by God. But the judgement of man's failure in the dispensation of grace is primary amongst its purposes. Indeed, as we shall see, man's failure in this dispensation does not even reach its fullest point until the Rapture takes place. 2 Thessalonians 2 informs us that tribulation judgement will follow upon a great apostasy – a rejection of the truth of Christianity, and the enthronement of a false god. It will be aimed particularly at those 'that perish; because they received not the love of the truth, that they might be saved' (v. 10). Their failure to believe not only took place in the dispensation of grace – before the Rapture and the onset of the Tribulation – but is linked closely with the way in which God is testing man in this dispensation. So, while this view is not without its own problems, on balance, I want to suggest that it accords best with the Biblical data. As such, it is the position that will be assumed in the remainder of this chapter.

REBELLION

As we have seen, man's responsibility in the dispensation of grace is, broadly speaking, twofold. God 'now commandeth all men every where to repent' (Acts 17:30) and mankind in general is responsible to respond to the gospel message, and to be baptised. Those who trust Christ are responsible to go into all the world and preach the gospel, to baptise those who believe, and to teach them to observe all that God has commanded. In both respects, man has failed.

The apostles and the early Christians were diligent and committed in their discharge of the great commission. Not for nothing were they known as 'these that turned the world upside down' (Acts 17:6). Their success in spreading the gospel was remarkable. But even as the gospel spread farther and farther, it became apparent that their work, and the work of the Holy Spirit through them, would not go unopposed. Many would refuse to believe on the Lord Jesus Christ for salvation. It is impossible for us to assess our own day in comparison with those that have gone before, but we know too well that, notwithstanding times of revival and blessing, the majority of those that hear the gospel refuse to submit to the command of the gospel, and will not believe on the Lord Jesus Christ.

Those whose rejection of the gospel was outright are only a part of man's failure in this dispensation. In the parables of the kingdom, in Matthew 13, the Lord Jesus highlighted a ploy that the Enemy of souls and of God would use to devastating effect:

> Another parable put He forth unto them, saying, The kingdom of heaven is likened unto a man which sowed good seed in his field: But while men slept, his enemy came and sowed tares among the wheat, and went his way. But when the blade was sprung up, and brought forth fruit, then appeared the tares also. So the servants of the householder came and said unto him, Sir, didst not thou sow good seed in thy field? from whence then hath it tares? He said unto them, An enemy hath done this. The servants said unto him, Wilt thou then that we go and gather them up? But he said, Nay; lest while ye gather up the tares, ye root up also the wheat with them. Let both grow together until the harvest: and in the time of harvest I will say to the reapers, Gather ye together first the tares, and bind them in bundles to burn them: but gather the wheat into my barn.
>
> Another parable put He forth unto them, saying, The kingdom of heaven is like to a grain of mustard seed, which a man took, and sowed in his field: Which indeed is the least of all seeds: but when it is grown, it is the greatest among herbs, and becometh a tree, so that the birds of the air come and lodge in the branches thereof.
>
> Another parable spake He unto them; The kingdom of heaven is like unto leaven, which a woman took, and hid in three measures of meal, till the whole was leavened (Mt. 13:24–33).

In these parables, the Lord provides us with an overview of what would happen in the sphere of Christian profession during the dispensation of grace. Each of these parables represents an effort to distort and pervert what is natural. They emphasise both the malevolent intent behind these efforts, and the secrecy with which they are performed. And they also present us with a progression. The first parable depicts the infiltration of the tares. These individuals were in the kingdom of heaven by virtue of their profession of faith in Christ. In reality, though, they were not genuine believers. Their presence was the fruit of a Satanic scheme, the work of 'an enemy'. In the second parable, we have an unnatural mutation. The growth described in this parable was neither natural nor healthy. It was certainly not in accordance with creatorial norms:

> And God said, Let the earth bring forth grass, the herb yielding seed, and the fruit tree yielding fruit after his kind, whose seed is in itself, upon the earth: and it was so. And the earth brought forth grass, and herb yielding seed after his kind, and the tree yielding fruit, whose seed was in itself, after his kind: and God saw that it was good (Gen 1:11–12).

A herb that becomes a tree is not part of God's design. This parable does not depict the burgeoning triumph of the Church. It rather portrays the unnatural, unhealthy ballooning of a Christendom that is marked by a mixture of profession and reality. Such an unnatural hybrid provides shelter for those fowls of the air, whose connotations in Scripture are always negative, if not Satanic. In the third parable, stealth and corruption are again foregrounded. Once more, we can draw on the wider Scriptural treatment of leaven as that which corrupts (*cf.* Lev. 2:11; Mk 8:15; 1 Cor. 5:6; Gal 5:9). In this parable, the leaven is concealed, surreptitiously and silently corrupting the three measures of meal.

Even a cursory reading of Church history will confirm for us the accuracy of the picture presented in these parables. The faithfulness and blessedness of the early Church proved largely impervious to direct opposition and persecution. Very soon, however, its ranks were swelled by those who were merely professors. Soon, the Church became an institution, and then an empire, rooted in the earth, and providing a home, and a legitimising cover for all evil. Christ had promised that He would build His Church, and that 'the gates of Hell shall not prevail against it' (Mt. 16:18). Nonetheless, the history of the dispensation of grace has been marked by a sad failure in separation and a dismal departure from purity.

It is important to notice that this departure has not yet reached its ultimate climax. 2 Thessalonians 2 is of crucial importance in this connection. In that chapter, Paul reveals that the full efflorescence of the mystery of iniquity, and its consequent judgement are being restrained:

> And now ye know what withholdeth that he might be revealed in his time. For the mystery of iniquity doth already work: only He who now letteth will let, until He be taken out of the way (vv. 6–7).

These verses have been interpreted in a number of different ways, and a variety of identifications have been suggested for the Withholder or Restrainer of whom they speak. Some commentators have suggested that the Roman Empire is in view, others that the verses speak of the restraint provided by civil society, the forces of law and order. Yet others have identified Satan as the Withholder, and at least one commentator has taken the unusual view that he is the Archangel Michael.* Our understanding of the verses will be greatly assisted if we note that they present us with a withholding person ('He who now letteth'), and a withholding 'what', designated by a neuter pronoun. The most satisfactory understanding of the verses is that the 'Who' is the Holy Spirit, presently dwelling on earth, within the believers of this dispensation. The 'what' refers to the Church, which is indwelt by the Holy Spirit. The Rapture, 'the coming of our Lord Jesus Christ, and ... our gathering together unto Him' (v.1) will accomplish the removal of the Church, and the Holy Spirit will no longer have the special dwelling place on earth that has been His throughout the dispensation of grace. The removal of these withholding agents 'out of the way' will allow the mystery of iniquity to rampage freely.

Its unbridled workings will be marked first by a great apostasy – *the* falling away. We mourn at the present state of Christendom, and the blasphemous doctrines that are announced by those who 'have a name to live but are dead' (Rev. 3:1) make our blood run cold. But even the current calamitous state of professing Christianity does not represent the nadir of man's failure in the dispensation of grace. The apostasy – unparalleled and unprecedented – is yet to take place. That departure will set the scene for the acceptance of 'that man of sin ... the son of perdition; who opposeth and exalteth himself above all that is called God, or that is worshipped; so that he as God sitteth in the Temple of God, shewing himself that he is God' (vv.3–4). Those

---

* These views are discussed in Pentecost, *Things to Come*, 259-63 and in William R. Glass, 'Identification of the Restrainer in 2 Thessalonians 2:6-7', Unpublished M.Th. thesis, The Capital Bible Seminary, 1992. The position that these verses refer to Michael is outlined in Gregory P. Allen, 'The Identity of the Restrainer in 2 Thessalonians 2:6-7', *Evangelical Theological Society Papers*, 35.

who have stood for error will fall for it, judicially blinded by God, 'that they all might be damned who believed not the truth, but had pleasure in unrighteousness' (v.12). And thus, the greatest age in the history of this world, that has been distinguished by the unparalleled display of Divine grace to mankind, will end in abject human failure, in the repudiation of Christ and Christianity by those who once professed it. Christ will be rejected, and Antichrist enthroned.

Retribution

On that rebellion, Divine judgement will fall. And it would be easy to recount the terrors of those seven years, to ransack Matthew 24 and the book of Revelation for the cataclysmic outpouring of Divine wrath upon rebellious mankind. But nothing could convey the horror of those days so simply, and yet with such haunting effectiveness as the words, recorded in Matthew 24:21, of the One into whose lips grace was poured (Ps. 45:2):

> For then shall be great tribulation, such as was not since the beginning of the world to this time, no, nor ever shall be.

Those unspeakable days will all tend towards one great, climactic moment of judgement, spelling the utter and abject defeat of all those who arrayed themselves in rebellion against God and His Christ:

> And I saw heaven opened, and behold a white horse; and He that sat upon him was called Faithful and True, and in righteousness He doth judge and make war. His eyes were as a flame of fire, and on his head were many crowns; and He had a name written, that no man knew, but He Himself. And He was clothed with a vesture dipped in blood: and His

name is called The Word of God. And the armies which were in heaven followed Him upon white horses, clothed in fine linen, white and clean. And out of His mouth goeth a sharp sword, that with it He should smite the nations: and He shall rule them with a rod of iron: and He treadeth the winepress of the fierceness and wrath of Almighty God. And He hath on His vesture and on His thigh a name written, King Of Kings, And Lord Of Lords. And I saw an angel standing in the sun; and He cried with a loud voice, saying to all the fowls that fly in the midst of heaven, Come and gather yourselves together unto the supper of the great God; that ye may eat the flesh of kings, and the flesh of captains, and the flesh of mighty men, and the flesh of horses, and of them that sit on them, and the flesh of all men, both free and bond, both small and great. And I saw the beast, and the kings of the earth, and their armies, gathered together to make war against Him that sat on the horse, and against His army. And the beast was taken, and with Him the false prophet that wrought miracles before Him, with which He deceived them that had received the mark of the beast, and them that worshipped his image. These both were cast alive into a lake of fire burning with brimstone. And the remnant were slain with the sword of Him that sat upon the horse, which sword proceeded out of His mouth: and all the fowls were filled with their flesh (Rev. 19:11–21).

CHAPTER 13

THE DISPENSATION OF THE FULNESS OF TIMES

THE TRUTH OF the Millennium – the thousand year earthly reign of the Lord Jesus Christ – is amongst the most controversial in Scripture. Throughout the history of Christianity, its reality, nature, and timing have all been debated. All this controversy has taken place in spite of the clarity with which the truth is stated in the Word of God:

> Blessed and holy is he that hath part in the first resurrection: on such the second death hath no power, but they shall be priests of God and of Christ, and shall reign with Him a thousand years (Rev. 20:6).

Revelation 20 is the only Scripture that explicitly refers to this reign of one thousand years, but throughout Scripture we find many more details about the nature of that reign, the conditions that will obtain and the rule that will operate throughout this glorious final dispensation.

Indeed, as we consider the truth of the Millennium a little more deeply, we come to realise not only that Scripture teaches that there will be a Millennium, but that there must be a Millennium. In Ephesians 1:10, Paul refers to the Millennium as 'the dispensation of the fulness of times'. We have already seen that the dispensation of grace is the climax of history, now we learn that the Millennium is the completion of history. At present, there are many loose ends in the purposes of God. In the Millennium, each and every thread will be taken up, and woven into God's great historical tapestry, for 'there are with Him no loose or broken ends.'[*]

Foremost amongst the purposes of the Millennium will be the vindication of Christ. The world saw Him, bearing the mockery and the opprobrium of Jew and Gentile, nailed to a cross. That cross was to the Jew a symbol of one accursed; to the Gentile it indicated a felon so base, so contemptible that only the agonising and shameful death of a rebellious slave was good enough. Though the apostles preached the resurrection and ascension of Christ, for many that verdict has never been reversed: our Lord is still rejected and disowned. His precious name is traduced and blasphemed, His character attacked, His person denied. But God has taken account of every claim made against His Son and, on the earth where He was rejected, and amongst those who rejected Him, Christ will be vindicated. God will have the last word as to the righteousness, holiness, and greatness of His beloved Son. God's time is set when He will show His Son as 'the blessed and only Potentate, the King of kings, and Lord of lords' (1 Tim. 6:15). Christ humbled Himself; God will exalt Him and 'at the name of Jesus every knee should bow ... and every tongue ... confess that Jesus Christ is Lord, to the glory of God the Father' (Phil. 2:10–11). 'Upon this earth, where the Son of man has been in humiliation, the Son of man shall be glorified. If this earth in itself is but a small thing, that

---

[*] Winifred A. Iverson, 'The Lord will perfect that which doth concern me', *Believers Hymn Book*, (Kilmarnock: John Ritchie, 1996), No. 453.

which God has done upon it, and will do, is not a small thing for Him.'*

The Millennium is also of crucial importance to God's plan for Israel. We have traced some of the promises that God made to Abraham, Isaac, and Jacob. Those promises await their fulfilment. But they have not been broken, and cannot be, for 'the gifts and calling of God are without repentance' (Rom. 11:29). God will keep His promises to Israel, and His purpose in choosing and calling her will be achieved, as she takes up her position as the head of the nations, and not the tail (Deut. 28:13). Under the restoring hand of God, and in repentance for her sin, she will become 'an eternal excellency, a joy of many generations' (Isa. 60:15).

For the nations, the Millennium will be a period of righteous rule. Christ Himself will be King, and through His people He will administer the planet in absolute righteousness. The world has never seen this. We have seen how every dispensation is marked and marred by human failure. Every system of government is likewise marked by unrighteousness because it is operated by unrighteous men. What a difference there will be when 'the government shall be upon His shoulder' (Isa. 9:6). Isaiah 32 outlines for us a golden future for this earth that all takes character from the first verse – 'Behold, a king shall reign in righteousness.' That righteous Head will impose His righteous rule: 'a sceptre of righteousness is the sceptre of [His] kingdom' (Heb. 1:8).

For Creation, Christ's reign will be a time of deliverance. Romans 8:22 is stating evident truth when it says 'we know that the whole Creation groaneth and travaileth in pain together until now.' Adam's fall was a disaster for mankind, but the ripples of its cataclysmic

---

* J. N. Darby, *The Collected Writings of J.N. Darby*, ed. William Kelly, (Sunbury, PA: Believers Bookshelf, 1971), 2:289.

effects have spread through all Creation. Once the pristine product of the hand of God, it is presently 'in the bondage of corruption' (Rom. 8:21). But as Christ reigns, Creation will be delivered from the stunting and deforming effects of sin, to declare, as never since the fall, the glory of God the Creator. Christ's redeeming work has paid the price for the believer, body, soul, and spirit. But His work goes far beyond that, and the cosmic effects of His redemption will one day be seen as He reigns.

But what of the Church in all of this? Is it her lot, as some have suggested, to sit in isolation from all of these events on earth, so happy in her heavenly security as to have no interest in the reign of Christ on earth? Scripture refutes this – the hope of the Millennium is a hope of the Church and of the believer no less than the Rapture, and we will have our part to play in Christ's triumphant reign.

Firstly, for the Church, it will be a time of revelation. In Romans 8:18 Paul weighs present and future and declares 'that the sufferings of this present time are not worthy to be compared with the glory which shall be revealed in us.' In the next verse, he links the deliverance of Creation with 'manifestation of the sons of God'. The Millennium, then, will be a time when the glorified Church, redeemed and cleansed by Christ's precious blood, will be revealed to Creation as the crowning glory of God's great master plan. It has ever been His purpose that 'in the ages to come He might shew the exceeding riches of His grace in His kindness toward us through Christ Jesus' (Eph. 2:7). And we will declare not only His grace, but His glory: 'when He shall come to be glorified in His saints, and to be admired in all them that believe ... in that day' (2 Thess. 2:10). Those who have trusted Christ in the dispensation of grace will be the perfect revelation of His grace and His glory in His Millennial kingdom.

The Millennium will also be a time of reigning for the Church. The very verse that promises that Christ will reign associates His people with that rule: 'Blessed and holy is he that hath part in the first resurrection: on such the second death hath no power, but they shall be priests of God and of Christ, and shall reign with him a thousand years' (Rev. 20:6). This is the great climax of grace – those gathered around the freshly-slain Lamb sing, as the very high-point and apotheosis of their worship of the One Who has 'made us unto our God kings and priests: and we shall reign on the earth' (Rev. 5:10). The Lord Jesus will not require our assistance to administer this world, He is capable of bearing all of its government, in all of its complexity, on a single shoulder. But in grace, His purpose for His Church is that they should share in His righteous reign. This hope is one of the vital threads linking our present with our future for, it has been truly said, our present life is 'training for reigning' – 'if we suffer, we shall also reign with Him' (2 Tim. 2:12).

But, above all else, the Millennium will be a time of rejoicing for the Church. She will not rejoice alone: this is 'the marriage supper of the Lamb' when her joy will be shared by Israel, by the nations, and by Creation itself. All will rejoice in the great and glorious consummation of the purposes of God for His own, but how uniquely sweet will be the joy of the Bride, united with the Beloved, transformed to His likeness, displayed as the fruit *par excellence* of His suffering, and manifesting His grace and glory to a wondering world. This will be the achievement of the believer's every hope, the culmination and the climax of the work of God's grace in our lives.

This is the dispensation of the fulness of times – every strand of God's purpose will achieve its full fruition. God's greatness and wisdom will be manifest, and a wondering world will learn that He was in control all along, and that His way was best. The Millennium is a thousand-year-long celebration of the triumph of Christ, a vivid demonstration of the failure of all of Satan's spoils and stratagems. Throughout this glorious age, he will watch, bound and impotent, as his plans unravel, as his schemes disintegrate, and as the world is freed from his baleful influence.

REVELATION

The keynote of revelation in the Millennium is the manifestation of Jesus Christ. His first coming was shrouded in relative obscurity, a secret to all but a few. His coming to the air for the Church will take place secretly – only those who rise 'to meet the Lord in the air' (1 Thess. 4:17) will see Him. But as He is manifest in His triumphant return, He will be visible to all:

> Behold, He cometh with clouds; and every eye shall see Him, and they also which pierced Him: and all kindreds of the earth shall wail because of Him (Rev. 1:7).

His glory will be 'as the lightning cometh out of the east, and shineth even unto the west' (Mt. 24:27), unmissable and unmistakable, impossible to counterfeit or to ignore. And as His kingdom is established, its grandeur will manifest the greatness of God in every nook and cranny of Creation:

> They shall not hurt nor destroy in all my holy mountain: for the earth shall be full of the knowledge of the LORD, as the waters cover the sea (Isa. 11:9).

> For the earth shall be filled with the knowledge of
> the glory of the LORD, as the waters cover the sea
> (Hab. 2:14).

The torn and tattered scroll of Creation will be repaired. Nature will once again present its primeval testimony to the greatness, the glory, and the goodness of God.

At this time, too, Israel will enter into the enjoyment of the blessings of the new covenant. Those blessings will have their effect in a place untouched by all the earlier covenants made by God with mankind:

> This shall be the covenant that I will make with the house of Israel; After those days, saith the Lord, I will put My law in their inward parts, and write it in their hearts; and will be their God, and they shall be My people. And they shall teach no more every man his neighbour, and every man his brother, saying, Know the Lord: for they shall all know Me, from the least of them unto the greatest of them, saith the Lord: for I will forgive their iniquity, and I will remember their sin no more (Jer. 11:33–34).

The finger of God will reach into the repentant hearts of His ancient people, and, in contrast to the external and emphasised phylacteries that they had worn in an earlier dispensation, will inscribe His Word within them.

Israel will not hold that revelation to herself. Instead, she will fulfil the purpose that God always had in mind for her. She will become, at last, a priestly nation, modelling the character of God to a wondering world. So signal will her blessing be that men and women from every part of the globe will make their pilgrimage to Jerusalem to learn of God, and to share His blessings:

> Thus saith the LORD of hosts; It shall yet come to pass, that there shall come people, and the inhabitants of many cities: And the inhabitants of

one city shall go to another, saying, Let us go speedily to pray before the LORD, and to seek the LORD of hosts: I will go also. Yea, many people and strong nations shall come to seek the Lord of hosts in Jerusalem, and to pray before the LORD. Thus saith the Lord of hosts; In those days it shall come to pass, that ten men shall take hold out of all languages of the nations, even shall take hold of the skirt of him that is a Jew, saying, We will go with you: for we have heard that God is with you (Zech. 8:20–22).

In this great age, for Israel, and for the world, the words of Isaiah's prophecy will come to pass:

> For the LORD is our judge, the LORD is our lawgiver, the LORD is our king (Isa. 33:22).

Responsibility

In the light of this revelation, those who live in the Millennium have a clear responsibility to obey the Divine law, and to live by its righteous standard. In her function as a priestly nation, Israel will be responsible for the service of God. In the rebuilt and restored Temple, animal sacrifices will, once again, be offered (Ezek. 46). The structure and ceremony of the Jewish religious year will be restored, and the feasts of Jehovah will annually unfold a retrospective survey of God's dealings with mankind (Ezek. 45). Indeed, attendance at Jerusalem for the feast of tabernacles will be obligatory for the nations, and failure to present themselves there will be met with severe judgement:

> And it shall come to pass, that every one that is left of all the nations which came against Jerusalem shall even go up from year to year to worship the King, the LORD of hosts, and to keep the feast of

> tabernacles. And it shall be, that whoso will not come up of all the families of the earth unto Jerusalem to worship the King, the LORD of hosts, even upon them shall be no rain. And if the family of Egypt go not up, and come not, that have no rain; there shall be the plague, wherewith the LORD will smite the heathen that come not up to keep the feast of tabernacles. This shall be the punishment of Egypt, and the punishment of all nations that come not up to keep the feast of tabernacles (Zech. 14:16–19).

These religious services cannot be a mere veneer on vice, or, as they so often have been, an attempt to conceal unrighteousness and evil. Rather, they are to be underpinned by an inflexible commitment to Divine righteousness in all areas of life. This correlation emerges very clearly in the context of the directions for the offerings given by God to Ezekiel:

> Thus saith the Lord GOD; Let it suffice you, O princes of Israel: remove violence and spoil, and execute judgment and justice, take away your exactions from My people, saith the Lord GOD. Ye shall have just balances, and a just ephah, and a just bath. The ephah and the bath shall be of one measure, that the bath may contain the tenth part of a homer, and the ephah the tenth part of a homer: the measure thereof shall be after the homer. And the shekel shall be twenty gerahs: twenty shekels, five and twenty shekels, fifteen shekels, shall be your maneh (Ezek. 45:9–12).

These units of quotidian trade are the units that God is about to use to define the offerings required in His service. Injustice to man would translate directly into insult to God. The writings of the prophets redound with warnings against corruption and unrighteousness, and these warnings will not have lost their relevance in the Millennial age. But now they will come to people with changed hearts, and the prayer of Amos will at last be answered:

> But let judgment run down as waters, and righteousness as a mighty stream (Amos 5:24).

Rebellion

It is important to remember that all those who enter the Millennium will have passed through the judgement of the living nations described in Matthew 25:

> When the Son of man shall come in His glory, and all the holy angels with Him, then shall He sit upon the throne of His glory: and before Him shall be gathered all nations: and He shall separate them one from another, as a shepherd divideth His sheep from the goats: and He shall set the sheep on His right hand, but the goats on the left. Then shall the King say unto them on His right hand, Come, ye blessed of my Father, inherit the kingdom prepared for you from the foundation of the world: for I was an hungred, and ye gave Me meat: I was thirsty, and ye gave Me drink: I was a stranger, and ye took Me in: naked, and ye clothed Me: I was sick, and ye visited Me: I was in prison, and ye came unto Me (Mt. 25:31–36).

As was the case so long ago with Rahab, the attitude of these individuals to God's witnesses, evidenced by their kindness at considerable personal danger, demonstrated their faith in God. Only these righteous enter into the Millennial kingdom, the rest depart 'into everlasting fire' (v.41).

The Millennium, then, commences with a redeemed and righteous people on a restored and resplendent earth. Furthermore, at the commencement of the dispensation, Satan will have been shut up and sealed in the bottomless pit (Rev. 20:2–3), and thus mankind will be free from his incitements to sin. In these circumstances, it is hardly surprising that sin will be exceptional.

In spite of all the blessings of Christ's reign, however, fallen human nature is inveterately sinful. Even without Satanic promptings, and even in the perfect social conditions that will prevail, man will still have a propensity to sin. Those born during the Millennium will not be automatically regenerate, and in this dispensation as in all others, salvation will still be availed of on the principle of faith. Thus, while sin will be unusual, it will not be absent.

Open rebellion against the Law of God will be promptly punished. The blessings of the Millennium will bring great longevity to mankind, and premature death will be a token of Divine judgement on sin:

> There shall be no more thence an infant of days, nor an old man that hath not filled his days: for the child shall die an hundred years old; but the sinner being an hundred years old shall be accursed (Isa. 65:20).

Judgement will be swift, just, and transparent. So clear will the link between sin and its punishment be that it will be futile to attempt to shift the blame on to anyone or anything else:

> In those days they shall say no more, The fathers have eaten a sour grape, and the children's teeth are set on edge. But every one shall die for his own iniquity: every man that eateth the sour grape, his teeth shall be set on edge (Jer. 31:30).

In light of the fact that such judgement will inevitably fall upon disobedience, it is hardly surprising that open rebellion during the Millennium will be exceptional. Fear of God, in the absence of any higher motive, will command the respectful obedience and submission of all. Indeed, it will appear that all of mankind's problems have at last been solved. But the root of all man's problems will still be there, and even this dispensation will ultimately be stained with the scarlet of human rebellion. Revelation 20 describes the course that this rebellion will take:

> And when the thousand years are expired, Satan shall be loosed out of his prison, and shall go out to deceive the nations which are in the four quarters of the earth, Gog, and Magog, to gather them together to battle: the number of whom is as the sand of the sea. And they went up on the breadth of the earth, and compassed the camp of the saints about, and the beloved city (Rev. 20:7–9).

Even after one thousand years of righteous rule, even in the face of God's goodness displayed in Creation, Satan will still find listening ears and open hearts. He will rally them to his standard, and muster them in one last desperate and doomed rebellion against God and His Christ, and against the nation that he hates.

The Millennium is the dispensation of the fulness of times, and as it brings God's every purpose to completion, so too it completes the sad history of human failure. Ever since Eden man has sinned. And, ever since Eden, he has tried to place the blame of that sin on something external to himself. It is society's fault, or genetics, or upbringing. This final rebellion gives the lie to every vainly exculpatory attempt. This rebellion, this arrant display of astonishing ingratitude can only be accounted for by man's sin, his inveterate desire to dethrone God, and to set something – anything – up in His place.

Retribution

Man's final rebellion is met by God's final retribution:

> And fire came down from God out of heaven, and devoured them. And the devil that deceived them was cast into the lake of fire and brimstone, where the beast and the false prophet are, and shall be tormented day and night for ever and ever (Rev. 20:9–10).

This final climactic judgement brings time to a close, as Creation itself is dissolved:

> But the day of the Lord will come as a thief in the night; in the which the heavens shall pass away with a great noise, and the elements shall melt with fervent heat, the earth also and the works that are therein shall be burned up (2 Pet. 3:10).

All the works of man are cleared away, and in the space that remains is set up the Great White Throne:

> And I saw a great white throne, and Him that sat on it, from Whose face the earth and the heaven fled away; and there was found no place for them. And I saw the dead, small and great, stand before God; and the books were opened: and another book was opened, which is the book of life: and the dead were judged out of those things which were written in the books, according to their works. And the sea gave up the dead which were in it; and death and hell delivered up the dead which were in them: and they were judged every man according to their works. And death and hell were cast into the lake of fire. This is the second death. And whosoever was

not found written in the book of life was cast into the lake of fire (Rev. 20:11-15).

This final judgement not only brings this dispensation to a close. All of human history is brought to an end, and eternity begins. For those whose names are not found written, that eternity will be filled with unending anguish. For those who have been saved, by grace and through faith, in each of God's great dispensational ages, a home is provided in the new heaven and a new earth that will be unveiled. Throughout eternity, the citizens of the eternal state will be occupied in the service and worship of God. A perfect administration will mark this eternal state. God will still have things to teach His own. But the testing is done, the dispensational lessons have all been learned. As we spend eternity wondering at the glories of our God, we will surely look back, with a perfect perspective and wonder at the way in which He shaped the history of this world to the accomplishment of His purpose and the amplification of His glory.

I'll bless the hand that guided,
I'll bless the heart that planned,
When throned where glory dwelleth,
In Immanuel's land.

Anne Ross Cousin

Chapter 14

Conclusion

THE EPISTLE TO the Galatians is the most urgently expressed of Paul's letters. Paul has hardly expressed his customary salutations before he turns his attention to the problem that had emerged in the Galatian church. That problem was so serious and so fundamental as to require the full force and censure of the apostle's authority. So, scarcely had the ink dried on his opening words before he expressed his amazement and dismay that the Galatians were 'so soon removed' to 'another gospel' (Gal. 1:6). And, as the epistle unfolds, Paul outlines the nature of this 'other gospel', and cuts right to the heart of the Galatian problem:

> O foolish Galatians, who hath bewitched you, that ye should not obey the truth, before whose eyes Jesus Christ hath been evidently set forth, crucified among you? This only would I learn of you, Received ye the Spirit by the works of the law, or by the hearing of faith? Are ye so foolish? having begun in the Spirit, are ye now made perfect by the flesh? (Gal. 3:1–3).

The Galatian believers were getting their dispensations confused. Having trusted Christ in the dispensation of grace, they were looking back with a misplaced nostalgia at the ceremony and strictures of the dispensation of Law, and, rather than standing fast 'in the liberty wherewith Christ hath made us free', they were becoming 'entangled again with the yoke of bondage' (Gal. 5:1). Their lack of dispensational clarity had a tremendous impact on every aspect of their lives, and on their understanding of Christ, the cross, and the gospel. And so the Apostle writes, with striking vigour, to adjust their thinking and to correct their defective dispensational comprehension.

Similarly, in his first letter to the church at Corinth the Apostle Paul had to correct a range of serious and urgent problems. The Corinthians' intellectual pride, their partisan praising of God's servants, and their lack of moral perception are all addressed by the apostle. These problems resulted, in large part, from the Corinthians dispensational dyslexia. Notwithstanding their vaunted knowledge, they had confused the order of the Divine programme, and were reigning 'as kings' (1 Cor. 4:8), anticipating the inauguration of the Millennium even as the apostles grappled in mortal combat with the god of this age.

As in the Galatian epistle, Paul makes it very clear that this lack of dispensational clarity was no mere intellectual problem. Rather, it lay at the root of some of the pressing practical problems in the church at Corinth. There is, of course, nothing unusual in this. Doctrine always matters, and error there will inevitably manifest itself in our behaviour. It is, however, important to stress this, for dispensational truth is often depicted as an arid channel of scriptural speculation that may not be actually dangerous, but is of little value to understanding Scripture, or living a Christian life.

This view is relatively widespread, but it could not be more mistaken. A grasp of the dispensational framework prevents us from imitating the errors of the

Conclusion

Galatians or the Corinthians. It allows us to achieve a proper perspective on God's dealings with mankind. And it unlocks the value of all of Scripture. It allows the Old Testament and the New to speak in their proper register, and to rhyme perfectly with each other. And it reveals to us, with renewed force, the unimaginable and inexhaustible greatness of our God.

Our study of the dispensations has taken us – far too quickly and superficially – through the ages of history. It has required us to look, albeit in a cursory way, at a wide range of Scriptures. And it has brought before us again and again the glory and the grace of God. We have been reminded too of the inveterate failure of man. We cannot contemplate this without sadness, but, equally, we cannot but wonder at the way in which God weaves even these dark and doleful threads into the pattern He has planned.

This is only an introductory study. The reformers were fond of quoting Gregory I's observation that the Word of God 'is as it were, a kind of river, which is both shallow and deep, wherein both the lamb may find a footing, and the elephant float at large.' We have been more like paddling lambs than wallowing elephants in this study, but we have ventured far enough to confirm that the water is balmy and inviting, refreshing to the mind and to the soul. It is my prayer that all who have journeyed through these pages will leave them with a renewed desire to launch out from these shallow waters into the bracing depths of God's unfailing Word.

Bibliography

The sections of this bibliography are arranged, as far as possible, in the order in which the subjects covered arise in this book. Inclusion of a work in the bibliography does not indicate an endorsement of the author's work in its entirety.

Dispensationalism

CHAFER, Lewis Sperry. *Systematic Theology, Vol. 4*. Grand Rapids, MI: Kregal, 1976.

CHAFER, Lewis Sperry *Major Bible Themes*. Available online at http://www.davidcox.com.mx/library/C/Chafer/chafer_major_bible_themes_18.htm, accessed 14 June 2012.

DUNLAP, David. *The Glory of the Ages*. Marne, MI: Gospel Folio Press, 2008.

PENTECOST, J. Dwight, *Things to Come: A Study in Biblical Eschatology*. Grand Rapids, MI: Zondervan, 1965.

RYRIE, Charles. *Dispensationalism*, Chicago, IL: Moody Press, 2007.

SAUER, Erich. *From Eternity to Eternity: An Outline of the Divine Purposes*. London: Paternoster, 1957.

TOLL, J.G., 'The Ages', *Present Truth*. Vol. 1 & 2. 1984–5.

History of Dispensationalism

COAD, F. Roy. *A History of the Brethren Movement*. (2nd ed.). Exeter: Paternoster, 1976.

MANGUM, Todd and Mark S. Sweetnam. *The Scofield Bible: Its History and Impact on the Evangelical*

Church. Colorado Springs, CO: Paternoster, 2009.

STUNT, Timothy C.F. 'Influences in the early development of J. N. Darby' in Crawford Gribben and Timothy C. F. Stunt, eds. *Prisoners of Hope? Aspects of Evangelical Millennialism in Britain and Ireland, 1800–1880.* Carlisle: Paternoster, 2004.

———.'John Nelson Darby: contexts and perceptions' in Crawford Gribben and Andrew R. Holmes, eds., *Protestant Millennialism, Evangelicalism and Irish Society, 1790–2005.* Basingstoke: Palgrave Macmillan, 2006, 83–98.

———. *From Awakening to Secession: Radical Evangelicals in Switzerland and Britain, 1815–35.* Edinburgh: T & T Clark, 2000.

SWEETNAM, Mark S. and Crawford Gribben. 'J. N. Darby and the Irish origins of dispensationalism'. *Journal of the Evangelical Theological Society.* 52:3 (2009), 569–577.

DICTIONARIES

MOUNCE, William. *Mounce's Complete Expository Dictionary of Old and New Testament Words.* Grand Rapids, MI: Zondervan, 2006.

VINE, W.E. *An Expository Dictionary of New Testament Words.* London: Oliphant, 1961.

COMMENTARIES ON HEBREWS

BRUCE, F.F. *Commentary on the Epistle to the Hebrews : the English text.* London : Marshall, Morgan & Scott, 1974.

FLANIGAN, J.M. *What the Bible Teaches – Hebrews.* Kilmarnock : J. Ritchie, 1991.

GUTHRIE, Donald. *The Letter to the Hebrews: an introduction and commentary.* Leicester: Intervarsity Press, 1983.

KELLY, William. *An Exposition of the Epistle to the Hebrews.* London: T. Weston, 1905.

WESTCOTT, Brooke Foss. *The Epistle To The Hebrews: The Greek Text with Notes and Essays* 2nd edition. London: Macmillan, 1892.

BIBLICAL COVENANTS

BARRICK, William D. 'The Mosaic covenant'. *TMSJ.* 10:2 (1999), 213–232.

ESSEX, Keith H. 'The Abrahamic covenant'. *TMSJ.* 10:2, (1999), 191–212.

LOPEZ, René. 'Israelite Covenants in the Light of Ancient Near Eastern Covenants (Part 1 of 2)'. *CTS Journal.* 9 (2003), 92–111.

———. 'Israelite Covenants in the Light of Ancient Near Eastern Covenants (Part 2 of 2)'. *CTS Journal.* 10 (2004), 72–106.

PETTEGREW, Larry D. 'The New Covenant'. *TMSJ.* 10:2, (1999), 251–270

ROGERS, Cleon L. 'The Covenant with Abraham and Its Historical Setting'. *Bibliotheca Sacra.* 127:507 (1970), 241–256.

———. 'The covenant with Moses and its historical setting'. *Journal of the Evangelical Theological Society.* 14:3 (2009), 569–577.

WEINFELD, M. 'The Covenant of Grant in the Old Testament and in the Ancient near East'. *Journal of the American Oriental Society.* 90:2 (1970), 184–203.

Commentaries on Genesis

KLEIN, Meredith. 'Genesis' in *The New Bible Commentary*, 3rd rev. D. Guthrie (ed.). Downers Grove, IL: Inter-Varsity Press, 1970, 79–114.

MCKEOWN, James. *Genesis*. Grand Rapids, MI: William B. Eerdmans, 2008.

PINK, A.W. *Gleanings in Genesis*. London : Wakeman Trust, 2011.

WENHAM, Gordan J. *Word Biblical Commentary, Vol. 1: Genesis 1–15*. Nashville, TN: Thomas Nelson, 1997.

Commentaries on Deuteronomy

MACKINTOSH, C.H. *Notes on the Book of Deuteronomy*. New York: Loizeaux Brothers, 1879.

THOMPSON, John Arthur. *Deuteronomy, an introduction and commentary*. London: Inter-varsity Press, 1974.

Siege of Jerusalem

JOSEPHUS, Flavius, *The Jewish Wars*. trans. William Whiston, BJ5.446. Available on-line at http://perseus.uchicago.edu/. (Accessed 20 June 2012).

MONTEFIORE, Simon Sebag. *Jerusalem: The Biography*. London: Weidenfeld & Nicolson, 2011.

TACITUS. *The Histories*. Ed. D.S. Levane. Oxford: Oxford University Press, 2001.

Daniel's Seventy Weeks

ANDERSON, Robert. *The Coming Prince*. Grand Rapids, MI: Kregel, 1952.

HOEHNER, Harold W. *Chronological Aspects of the Life of Christ*. Grand Rapids, MI: Zondervan, 1978.

Mystery Doctrines

HOSTE, William. *The Collected Writings: Volume 2 – Prophetic*. Kilmarnock: John Ritchie, 2004.

IRONSIDE, Harry A. *The Mysteries of God*. New York: Loizeaux Brothers, 1908.

VINE, W.E. *The Twelve Mysteries of Scripture*. London: Pickering and Inglis, n.d.

WILSON, T. Ernest. *Mystery Doctrines of the New Testament: God's Sacred Secrets*. Neptune, NJ: Loizeaux Brothers, 1975.

Parables of the Kingdom

PINK, A. W. *The Prophetic Parables of Matthew 13*. Available on-line at http://www.pbministries.org/books/pink/Parables/index.htm, (Accessed 15 June 2012.)

Scripture Index

Genesis

Reference	Page
1:2	82
1:7	120
1:11–12	210
1:26	100
1:31	89
2:8	90
2:16–17	92
2:18	103
2:21	152
3:1	96
3:4	97
3:5	97
3:6	98
3:4–7	113
3:14–15	104–105
3:15	30
3:16	95, 103
3:17–19	102
3:22	113
4:16	117
4:17	109
4:26	111
5:1–3	101
6:3	82, 112
6:5	117
6:6–7	118
6:7	121
6:8	111
6:9	122
6:11	135
6:13	121
6:18	123
7:11	119
7:19–23	121
8:21–22	129
9:7	131
9:11	132
9:12–16	132
10:5	49, 134
10:8–9	134
10:9	136
11	49
11:1–9	139
11:4	133, 147
12	49, 157
12:1	146
12:6	150
14	151
15	150
15:1–6	150
15:9–11	151
15:13–16	152
15:18	151
17	153
17:1–8	153–154
17:9–13	156
17:9–16	155
17:14	151
18:2	86

21:27	151
21:32	151
26:2–5	76
26:24	154
26:28	151
27:16	83
28:14–15	154
31:44	151
32:24–30	76
35:10–12	155
46:2–4	155
50:24	155

EXODUS

4:24–25	160
19	166, 173, 177
19:7–8	173
20:2–3	175
20:5	168
20:7	168
20:24	68
23:20–23	176
23:32	151
25:9	168
28:41	83
32:1	175
34:10	151
34:12	151
34:15	151

LEVITICUS

2:11	210
17:11	68
26	168
26:14–17	169
32	172

DEUTERONOMY

27–28	168
28	181
28:13	217
28:15–20	169
28:25	182
28:36–37	182
28:41	182
28:49–53	183
28:62–68	183–184
32	170, 172
32:46–47	170

JOSHUA

5:2–5	160
5:6	161

JUDGES

6:34	83
13:25	83
14:6	83–84
14:19	83–84

1 SAMUEL

26:12	152

1 CHRONICLES

12:18	83

2 CHRONICLES

36:15–16	77

JOB

4:13	152
33:14–17	76

33:15	152	18:20	67
38:7	90	33:2–6	92
40:4	93–94	36:22–28	85
		37:12–14	85

Psalms

2:1–2	140	45	222
8:4–8	101–102	45:9–12	223
19:1	61, 76	46	222
45:2	213		
48:2	165		

Daniel

9:24–27	203–204
11:32	98

51:11	83
85:10	195
107:31	24

Hosea

6:7	127

Proverbs

19:15	152

Joel

2:28–29	84

Isaiah

9:6	217
11:6–8	104
11:9	220
28:10	56
29:10	152
32	217
33:22	222
42:21	78
45:5	63
60:15	217
65:20	225

Amos

3:7–8	77
5:24	223

Micah

6:8	86

Habakkuk

2:4	70
2:14	220
3:2	99

Jeremiah

11:33–34	221
31:30	225
31:31–34	80, 196

Zechariah

8:20–22	222
14:16–19	223

Malachi

3:6	66

Ezekiel

Matthew

5:17	78
12:39	33
13	199, 208
13:24–33	209
13:39–40	28
13:49	28
16:18	192, 210
23:37–39	178
23:38	186
24	212
24:2	185
24:3	28
2:13	203, 206
24:13–15	203
24:20	203
24:21	52, 213
24:27	220
24:27–28	119
24:37–39	108
25:34	191
25:31–36	220, 224
26:28	50, 196
26:39	195
27:22–25	178–179
27:25	186
27:51	50
28:18–20	200
28:20	30

Mark

7:37	94
8:15	210
13:2	185
16:15	81
16:16	201

Luke

1:67–70	29
3:38	101
12	38–39
12:42	36, 39
12:45–46	39
13:34	77
13:35	186
16	38, 42
16:1	36
16:1–2	39
16:2	36
16:3	36
16:8	36
17:26–27	119
20	178
20:34	27
21:27	50
22:20	196
27:47	180

John

1	20
1:10–11	177
1:14	77, 195
1:15–18	78, 195
1:17	50
3:2–3	105
4:21–24	87
8:11	195
14:15	82
14:16	83
14:16–17	82
14:26	198
14:27	81

15:20–21	181	4:21	163
17:3	97	5:12	68, 99
17:17	82	5:19	95, 98
17:24	191	5:20	179
19:15	178	6:23	68
21:25	194	7:12	170
		8:3	172
ACTS		8:18	218
1:4–5	193	8:19–22	103
1:8	180	8:21	218
2:23	179	8:22	89, 217
2:40	33	9:4	197
2:42	198	10:4	50, 206
3:13–21	181	11:11–12	187
3:21	30	11:15	187
7:2	145	11:25	199
7:44	168	11:29	217
11:16	193	11:33	55, 93, 187
14:15–17	33	12:2	27
17:6	208	14:4	38
17:24–25	140	15:4	58
17:26	141	16:23	36
17:30	208	16:25	198
20:26	93	16:25–27	63
ROMANS		**1 CORINTHIANS**	
1:17	70	1:21	24
1:19–20	114	2:6–8	193
1:21	114	2:10	198
2:13–15	115	3:17	193
3:19	114	4:1	40
3:23–26	71	4:1–2	36
4:3	155	4:8	230
4:20	155	5:6	210
4:20–21	154		
6:19–20	193	9:17	36, 40

10:1–11	177
10:11	31, 190
11:10	96
11:25	196
13:8–10	79
15:20–22	100
15:22	105
15:24–28	60
15:51	199

2 Corinthians

3:6	196
3:18	105
4:6	58

Galatians

1:4	27
1:6	229
2:28	191
3:1–3	229
3:16–18	144
3:17	205
3:24	58, 171–172
4:2	36
5:1	230
5:9	210

Ephesians

1	42, 62
1:3–6	61
1:4	191
1:6	93
1:9	199
1:10	36, 51, 215
1:10–12	40
1:11	56
1:13	193
2:1–3	95
2:6	191
2:7	32, 218
2:8	122
2:11–13	197
2:14–16	197
2:19–22	79
2:20	198
3	42, 50, 198
3:2	36
3:2–7	41
3:4–5	34
3:9	36
3:14–15	94
3:20–21	33
5:32	198
6:12	191, 192
6:19	198

Philippians

2:10–11	216

Colossians

1	20, 33, 41–42
1:24–29	199
1:25–26	42
1:25	36, 40
1:26	30, 33
2:15	105, 206

1 Thessalonians

1:9	145
1:10	123
4:17	220
5:9	123

2 THESSALONIANS

2	207
2:4	203
2:6–7	211
2:7	199
2:10	218

1 TIMOTHY

1:4	36
1:17	24, 28
2:13	95
2:14	98
3:9	198
3:15	37
3:16	198
4:2	116
6:15	216

2 TIMOTHY

2:12	219
2:15	46
3:16	80

TITUS

1:7	36

HEBREWS

1:1	75
1:1–2	56, 77, 190
1:1–4	19–20, 194
1:2	28
1:3	58
1:8	217
2:7	98
2:14	105
3:5–6	37
3:8–11	162
3:12	159, 163
4	159
4:1	162
4:3	191
6:13–17	148–149
8:5	168
8:6	163
8:6–13	196
9:12–14	69
9:14	71
9:22	68
9:25	26
9:26	28, 190
10:1	71
10:4	71
10:12	71
11	112, 119
11:3	21
11:4	69
11:5	111, 123
11:6	70
11:7	111
11:8	146
11:11	155
12:1	112
12:18	49, 165
12:18–24	172–173
13:15	193

1 PETER

1:10–12	57
1:20	191
2:24	58
3:18	195

3:20	119	1:7	220
4:10	36, 40	1:20	198
		2:17	194
2 PETER		3:1	212
1:4	163	5:10	219
2:3–7	119	10:7	199
3:3–7	107	11:4	84
3:10	227	17–18	199
		19–20	198
1 JOHN		19:11–21	213–214
3:2–2	105	20:2–3	224
		20:6	215, 219
Jude		20:7–9	226
3	198	20:9–10	52, 226–227
		20:11–15	227
REVELATION			

Index

Abel, 58, 69, 71, 87, 108, 112, 116, 173
Abimilech, 157
Abraham, 21, 49, 51–52, 76, 86, 143–158, 161, 166, 181, 191, 217
Adah, 110
Adam, 21, 48, 51–52, 58, 63, 86, 90–105, 108–109, 113, 116, 120, 127, 152, 191, 217
ages, 13, 20–37, 41–44, 47, 55–56, 58–60, 62, 68–70, 79, 81, 83, 86, 90, 109, 190–191, 199, 218, 227, 231
Antichrist, 138, 212
apostasy, 207, 212
Assyria, 183
Babel, 49, 51, 134, 136–141, 147
Babylon, 137–138, 177, 183, 199
book of life, 227
Burns, Robbie, 62
Cain, 58, 69, 71, 108–110, 112, 116–117, 122
Calvary, 50, 57–58, 71, 105, 165, 179–180, 195, 205–206, 216, 230
Calvin, John, 61
Canaanites, 150–151

capital punishment, 130
Chafer, Lewis Sperry, 202–206
Christ, 19–22, 24, 26, 28, 30, 32–34, 37–38, 40–41, 50–51, 57–58, 61, 63, 68, 72, 79, 87, 96–97, 101, 108, 119, 165, 171–172, 176, 178, 186, 191, 193, 195, 197–199, 205, 210, 215, 217–220, 225–226, 229
ascension of, 216
blood of, 69, 71, 197, 218
character of, 78, 87, 216
Creator, 20, 21
death of, 28–29, 51, 70, 71, 72, 93, 129, 195
faith in, 208–209, 218, 229
first coming of, 29, 50, 191, 220
fulfilled law, 78
glory of, 171
greatness of, 216
humanity of, 105
Incarnation of, 29
mediator, 196
obedience of, 105
power of, 200

rejection of, 33, 52, 181, 186, 212–213, 216
resurrection of, 100
revelation in, 78, 194
righteousness of, 216
sacrifice of, 71
second coming of, 29, 123, 201, 211, 220
Son of God, 20, 58, 71, 177, 178, 190, 194
Son of man, 50, 108, 216, 224
sufferings of, 181
vindicated, 216
work of, 72, 87
Christendom, 88, 210, 212
Church, 32–33, 50, 65, 78–79, 84, 93, 173, 190–193, 199, 202, 206–207, 210–211, 218–220, 229–230
Bride of Christ, 192, 198, 219
circumcision, 151, 155–157, 160
conscience, 48, 57, 69, 72, 76, 107, 112–117, 181, 205
consummation of the ages, 21, 26, 28, 190, 203–205, 219
Cousins, Anne Ross, 23, 228
covenant, 49, 51, 80, 123, 127–129, 136, 149, 151–157, 159, 167, 172–173, 181, 183, 196–197, 204, 221, 235

Abrahamic, 149, 152–153, 155–156, 166
blessings, 144, 147
better, 163
cutting of, 151
Mosaic, 165–170, 191
blessings, 148, 153, 167–168, 170, 181
curses, 149, 166, 168–169, 181–182, 204
restated, 168
New, 80, 173, 195–197, 221
blessings, 61, 80, 84, 197, 221
New, 196
Noahic, 49, 126–128, 131–133, 135, 138
blessings, 130
obligatory, 166
promissory, 149
royal grant, 149, 166
suzerain, 166
covenant theology, 70
Creation, 20, 22, 37, 44–45, 49–50, 57, 61–63, 75–76, 82, 86, 89–90, 93, 95, 98, 99–104, 107–108, 110, 114–115, 118, 120, 129–130, 135, 143, 152, 165, 217–221, 226–227
culture, 141
Darby, John Nelson, 9, 24, 26, 77, 155, 217
David, 13, 21, 24, 29, 84
Day of Atonement, 22

devil. See Satan
dreams, 21, 79, 84
Eden, garden of, 48–49, 51, 65, 68, 75, 86, 90–91, 93–96, 100, 105, 109, 112, 127, 130, 171, 226
Egypt, 80, 158–162, 172, 175, 184, 223
Enoch, 109, 111, 123–124
Esau, 158
eternal state, 51, 228
Eve, 21, 48, 51–52, 58, 86, 92–102, 104, 108, 112–113, 116, 120, 152
Evolution, 22, 45, 108, 113
Fall, 48, 86, 91, 93, 95, 99–100, 105, 107, 109, 111, 113, 127, 130
feasts of Jehovah, 168, 171, 222
Fertile Crescent, 137
Flood, 49, 52, 119–124, 129, 133
fulness of times, 40, 42, 51, 216, 219, 226
generations, 30, 33–35, 42, 116, 119, 153, 156, 217
Gentiles, 41, 114–115, 134, 186–187, 197
giants, 122, 159
glorification, 20, 142
God
    changelessness of, 66–67
    character of, 19, 56, 58, 66–67, 73, 90, 94–95, 97–99, 114, 126, 162, 171, 221
    Creator, 22, 25, 28, 37, 39, 44, 90, 101, 114, 117, 126–127, 130, 138, 171, 210, 218
    El Shaddai, 154
    glory of, 19, 23–24, 32, 40, 50, 57–58, 60–63, 71, 76, 77, 81, 90–91, 94, 98, 101, 103, 105, 142, 144–146, 154, 163, 187, 193–194, 216, 218–221, 224, 228, 231
    grace of, 24, 32, 41, 56, 58, 61, 63, 67–68, 71, 76, 92, 94, 97, 105, 111, 119, 122–124, 126–128, 131–132, 147–149, 174, 179–181, 187, 189, 194–195, 212, 218–219, 227, 231
    greatness of, 62, 81, 101, 104, 114, 132, 167, 187, 219–221, 231
    power of, 19, 23, 30–32, 41, 50, 60, 62–63, 81, 85, 94, 100, 105, 111, 114, 117, 126, 129, 140, 144, 154, 171, 192, 194, 197, 200, 215, 219
    promise of, 167
    purpose of, 19–20, 22, 23, 26, 31–32, 36, 40, 45, 47, 52, 55–57, 60,–62, 72–73, 76, 81, 95,

105, 111, 129, 130–131, 133, 140–142, 144, 154, 162, 179, 189, 191, 197, 203, 217–219, 221, 226, 228
  righteousness of, 58, 67, 69, 71, 80, 82, 91, 94, 97–99, 111–112, 122, 126, 140, 150, 170, 174, 186, 195, 203–205, 213, 217, 219, 222–224, 226
  service of, 86–88, 94, 142, 144–145, 168, 171, 191, 193, 201, 205, 222, 223, 228
  sovereignty of, 44, 144, 147
gospel, 40–41, 57, 61, 63, 81, 99, 180, 200–201, 206, 208, 229, 230
  rejected, 181, 186, 208
Great Commission, 30, 200, 208
Great White Throne, 227
Hagar, 153, 158
Haran, 148, 150
history, 13, 21–26, 29, 31, 34–35, 42–44, 47–48, 51, 55, 60, 62, 65–67, 72, 80, 82, 105, 109, 110, 122, 128, 135, 138, 141, 143–144, 148, 165, 167, 171, 176, 186, 190, 193–195, 210, 212, 215–216, 226–228, 231
Holy Spirit, 69, 81–84, 86, 193, 229

  activity of, 85
  and creation, 82
  and inspiration, 19, 34, 57
  and revelation, 41
  baptism in, 193
  given, 50–51, 82, 189, 193
  indwelling, 79, 83, 85, 193, 229
  instructing, 197–198
  operation in O.T., 83–84
  operation in Tribulation, 84
  operation in Millennium, 84
  power of, 82, 86, 192
  presence of, 82
  promised, 82
  Restrainer, 84, 211
  seal of, 61, 193
  striving, 82, 112, 117
  wisdom of, 192
  work of, 82, 197, 208
human government, 130, 133, 136, 139, 142, 166
humanity, 44–45, 48–51, 58–59, 63, 72, 91–92, 94–95, 97–102, 104–105, 108, 110, 115–117, 127–128, 130, 133–135, 137–138, 140–142, 148, 170, 177
image of God, 19, 58, 71, 94, 100–101, 105, 189, 194, 214
Incarnation, 20, 29

inspiration, 29, 69, 76, 78, 80, 198
Isaac, 72, 76, 143, 154, 158, 181, 217
Israel, 29, 52, 65–66, 77, 80, 84–85, 87, 144, 157, 160–161, 166–167, 170, 172–175, 177, 181, 191–192, 196–197, 199, 203–207, 217, 219, 221–223
Jacob, 66, 76, 83, 143, 154, 158, 167, 181, 217
Jerusalem, 52, 58, 77, 87, 173, 178, 180, 184, 186, 189, 221–222, 236
  siege of, 52, 184, 202, 204
John the Baptist, 78, 194
Joseph, 76, 143, 154, 159, 185
Josephus, Flavius, 184–186
Jubal, 109
judgement, 39, 49, 52, 57, 68, 77, 82, 99, 108–109, 118–123, 126, 133, 138–141, 143, 161–162, 168, 177, 179, 180–181, 186, 201, 204, 206–207, 211–213, 222, 225, 227
judgement of the living nations, 224
Justification, 20
Kadesh-Barnea, 159, 161
kingdom of heaven, 208–209
Laban, 157
lake of fire, 52, 214, 226–227

Lamech, 109–110, 117
Last Supper, 196
Law, Mosaic, 49, 51, 65, 68–70, 76, 78, 165, 169–174, 179–180, 189, 195, 202, 204–206, 229
Levitical system, 52, 58, 68, 71
Lyte, Henry Francis, 73
Marduk, 137
marriage, 108–109, 127–128, 219
Messiah, 29, 52, 177–178, 186
Methuselah, 123
Millennium, 51–52, 80, 84, 90, 104, 191, 196–197, 201, 205, 207, 215–220, 222–226, 230
Moriah, 58
Mount Ararat, 125, 165
mystery doctrines, 29–30, 33–34, 41, 63, 84, 190, 192, 198, 212
mystery of iniquity, 211
nations, 30, 33–34, 49, 63, 134, 141–142, 153, 156–157, 177, 182–183, 191, 200, 213, 217, 219, 221–222, 224, 226
New Testament, 19, 21, 27, 36, 38, 79, 107, 120, 155, 158, 170–171, 193, 196, 198–199
Nimrod, 134, 135, 136, 138

Noah, 49, 51, 76, 108, 112, 118, 120–124, 126–128, 130–133, 135, 138, 165, 191
ark, 108, 118, 121–126, 132, 194
nomos, 36
oikonomeō, 36
oikonomia, 36, 38, 43
oikonomos, 36
oikonomos, 42
Oikos, 36, 38
Old Testament, 21–22, 24, 31, 70–71, 77, 78, 82, 84, 109, 127, 135, 152, 191, 203, 231
parables of the kingdom, 208
parenthesis, prophetic, 134, 190
Paul, 24, 30–34, 37–38, 40–42, 58, 78–79, 93, 114–115, 141, 144, 169, 170, 172, 176, 192, 196–197, 211, 215, 218, 229, 230
penal substitution, 57
Pentecost, day of, 50–51, 83–84, 193
Peter, 30, 33, 57, 84, 105, 107–108, 119, 145, 180, 192
Pharaoh, 157, 162
priesthood
Levitical, 168
promise, 30, 31, 41, 61, 76, 82, 85, 99, 105, 107, 123, 126–127, 131–132, 144, 147–150, 154, 155, 157–159, 161, 162–163, 166, 175, 192, 195, 197, 200, 202
prophecy, 19, 24, 29, 30, 34, 41, 57, 63, 77–79, 178, 181, 194, 198, 223
Rapture, 84, 111, 124, 199, 201, 206–207, 211, 218, 220
rebellion, 53, 95, 116, 133, 158, 174, 207, 224
relativism, 171
resurrection, 100, 202, 215–216, 219
retribution, 53, 99, 118, 139, 161, 180, 212, 226
revelation, 13, 20–23, 29–30, 34, 38, 41–45, 48–53, 55–58, 63, 70, 75–81, 84, 91–94, 112, 114–116, 126–127, 130–131, 133, 144, 154–155, 160, 166, 169, 170–171, 173–175, 193–196, 198–199, 206, 212, 218, 220–222, 226
Rome, 58, 183
Rowan, Ora, 145
sacrifice, 22, 26, 28, 57, 68–69, 72, 87, 112, 116, 128, 129, 146, 165, 171, 174, 180, 193
Levitical, 58, 71, 168, 171, 174, 223
sacrifice, 223
salvation, 29, 32, 51, 57, 61, 70–71, 73, 87, 122–123,

142, 172, 187, 190, 201, 208, 225
Sarah, 153–154, 156, 158
Satan, 27, 52, 95–100, 104–105, 111, 112–113, 115, 220, 224, 226
Sauer, Erich, 51
Scripture
  canon of, 79
seed of the woman, 29, 104, 111, 149, 153, 156
seed, promise of, 147, 152, 153
serpent, 29, 92, 95–96, 104, 105, 112
Seth, 101
Shinar, plain of, 137, 142
Sinai, 49, 52, 165, 172–173, 178, 189, 203–204
stewardship, 30, 36–40, 42, 45
substitutionary atonement, 58, 69
tabernacle, 22, 167
temple, 50, 52, 79, 86–87, 137, 138, 140, 185–186, 193, 203, 205, 212, 222
Ten Commandments, 168, 175
Tennyson, Arthur, Lord, 103
testing
  demonstrative, 59
  investigative, 59
Timothy, 37

Tribulation, 51, 84, 124, 201–206
Trinity, 47
Tubal-cain, 110
Tyndale, William, 53
visions, 21, 79, 84
Watts, Isaac, 72
worship, 32, 86–88, 115–116, 127, 145, 174–177, 193, 203, 219, 222, 228
Zachariah, 29, 30
Zillah, 110
Zipporah, 160

www.ingramcontent.com/pod-product-compliance
Lightning Source LLC
Chambersburg PA
CBHW062013220426
43662CB00010B/1314